T0338173

Best
Essays
NW

Best Essays NW

Perspectives from *Oregon Quarterly* Magazine

Guy Maynard &
Kathleen Holt,
Editors

UNIVERSITY OF
OREGON

PRESS

Eugene, Oregon

Published by:
University of Oregon Press
5283 University of Oregon
Eugene, OR 97403-5283
www.uopress.com

Designed by Jeffrey Jane Flowers
Interior photography by Jessica MacMurray

Printed in the United States of America.

ISBN: 0-87114-303-8

h g f e d c b a

Contents

Introduction

The sheer beauty of the place is almost enough: heroic mountains, open high desert, homey river valleys, rough and ragged coast, green and brown, blue and gray, sparkling and mysterious. Maybe that beauty alone can explain the draw of the great Oregon country (which runs from somewhere north of San Francisco to somewhere south of Alaska and most of the way east to the Rockies), why it's been able to attract and hold restless and hopeful immigrants for 10,000 years. But there's more. This remarkable landscape is given its soul by the stories that grow from it—stories as rooted in this place as fir trees and camas and blackberries and Oregon Grape. What a pleasure it's been for us, as editors of *Oregon Quarterly* magazine, to be the conveyors of some of these stories. And what a special delight to see the best of them compiled in this book, the Northwest perspective in all its variety and richness.

Oregon Quarterly is the magazine of the University of Oregon, sent to alumni and friends of the University of Oregon, but we are not "just" an alumni magazine. Our claim to be a regional magazine of ideas has never had a stronger proof than this collection of essays. Most of these essays have appeared in the magazine since 1994, when we shifted our mission to more consciously encompass the most important social, cultural, political and economic ideas affecting the Northwest—and to seek great writing about the region wherever we could find it, even when there weren't explicit ties to the University of Oregon.

In 2000, we took another step to seek and promote good writing about important ideas in the Northwest with the *Oregon Quarterly* Northwest Perspectives Essay Contest. It's open to anyone, with no entry fee, and the only subject limitation is that the essays relate somehow to ideas affecting the Northwest. In the contest's first three years, we attracted more than

200 entries from all over the Northwest and even from expatriates living in other parts of the United States. All the top three finishers (selected by Kim Stafford in 2000, Barry Lopez in 2001 and John Daniel in 2002) from those years are included here, as well as a selection of finalists we liked too much to leave out. The essay contest and the annual gathering where the winners read their essays have become genuine celebrations of all those who struggle to explore ideas through writing without much promise of fame and fortune. Barry Lopez's eloquent introduction to this volume is adapted from the remarks he made opening the 2001 reading.

And so, here are the stories that sprout from our corner of the world and the people who have been drawn to live here, from Kim Stafford's reflections on change and constancy in the Oregon country to John Daniel's thoughts about the science and mystery of human evolution. In between we read of berries and hawks, of the Coquille and the Nez Perce, of ranchers and loggers and millworkers, of rain and fire, of trains and frogs, of death and loss, of baseball and rowing, of war and welfare, of wind and grasses, of comings and goings—the stories of the Oregon country.

Guy Maynard
Kathleen Holt
November 2002

Foreword

In many traditional cultures, the single witness to a remarkable or uncommon event might not utter a word about that encounter until the right situation for relating the story arose. Such an occasion was usually social rather than private, and listeners with a range of experience were often included in the audience.

The witness would normally put forth the event in the way of a messenger, for the edification and consideration of the others—some of whom, the storyteller would know, might have had similar experiences. At that point (or later) someone (or no one) might comment. The important thing in relating the incident was not an analysis of its import or a consensus about its meaning; it was to continue the witness and to welcome the experience of others. Life, the storyteller would be implying, is unfathomable, and here is another example of it. And what do you think?

It is a reach to get from such a tribal setting, oral and communal, to the realm of the modern essay; but I believe the two are, at one level, similar. Both are attempts to convey something that is known or discovered by the storyteller; both are efforts to share emotional experience; and in both settings the storyteller must establish a trusting relationship with the listener. Where they differ most sharply is in what they hope to achieve. The emphasis in the former is on describing what happened; in the latter it's on urging the listener to see the world the way the storyteller does. To take this a step further, authority (our reason to listen) lies with the event in the one and with the storyteller in the other.

Over the past three or four decades, the essay has become a very popular form with American writers. Why? One good place to seek an answer, it seems to me, is with the compelling notion of modern disintegration.

We live—this is hardly news—in a highly fragmented time, an era of alarming personal and social disintegration. Many essayists, I believe, are writing in reaction to this state of affairs; they are arguing for, or trying to reason toward, forms of reintegration. In doing so, it seems to me the modern essayist is acting as much from social motives as upon artistic impulses.

What can we say makes for a good modern essay in this mode? I can think of three things at least. The best essays are distinguished by a search for meaning, by a disciplined effort to gain perspective on an issue, and by a willingness to make peace with the essential paradox of life. Life can't be straightened out, it can only by lived. We may be able to bring a measure of grace to it, but we must recognize that the direction our culture takes is not something always under our control. Still, even though it can't be fixed, a culture can be made less cruel, less harmful, indifferent or exploitative. And it is this, in my view, that many essayists are now trying to emphasize.

While an essay may well be compelled by such social feelings, and be driven by rational processes, I would also argue that the attempt to write a fine essay today is very like the effort to make good art. It is a striving for coherence, beauty, essence, epiphany, illumination and engagement both with the material and with the audience. To refine further on what is behind the impulse to work in this form, I want to look briefly at just two of its popular formats, the personal essay and the nature essay.

At its worst, the personal essay is solely about someone else's life or views; it carries no meaning for the rest of us. Often we can locate no point of entry, and but few points of identity. At its best, the personal essay tells the small story of the writer's life in such a way that the larger story of human life becomes clear. We can identify with the author's emotions, and we can accept his or her reflections as being similar to our own. The writer has done us a service by putting our vague misgivings or incomplete assessments of life into language. Having read the essay, we know more about the stance we wish to assume in the world.

At its best, the nature essay takes us outside cultural constructs and connects us with what the human imagination doesn't directly control—our biology. It connects us with our physical rather than our conceptual attachments to the world. By exploring our ecology—our relations with all that sustains us—it also brings in certain dimensions of anthropology, history and folklore. In short, it situates us outside the mind and the self.

The nature essay also seems to encourage at least two kinds of behavior that have atrophied in industrial cultures. One is the acceptance rather than the analysis of mystery, feeling not challenge but wonder in coming face-to-face with the profound. Second, the nature essay attempts to reawaken a sense of reciprocity with the world, which leads us away from the desire to own or dominate and toward feelings of generosity.

The topic of the nature essay, as I construe it, is not nature (instead, nature is its extended metaphor or central trope). It's good relations. Such essays are more often about the structure of prejudice, the inutility of hierarchy, the illusion (as Darwin saw it) of progress. The focal point of the nature essay is not nature apart from man, but the terrifying ground between ourselves and what lies outside the self.

What can we hope with the essays we read? We can hope that in reading good essays we will know better what we mean. We can hope that they will remind us to celebrate the richest dimensions of language, which do not have to do with the conveyance of information but rather with memory and layers of meaning. We can hope that they will alert us in startling ways to the idea that language is not a technology, that its essence is more akin to an animal's, biological rather than mechanical. And because it is, our relationship with it has a moral dimension. (If this sounds recondite, consider how the notion of telling a lie has been eclipsed over the last three or four decades. In public life today, we expect to hear the lies that will make us comfortable. The truth is less relevant. When language is viewed as a technology, the speaker simply "reprograms" a failed sentence until it achieves the desired result. The moral dimension is not paramount, or sometimes even important.)

We can also hope, finally, that the essays we read will take care of us. As personal as the views may be, we can still ask, I think, that the writers be thoughtful about us. The world remains wondrous and perilous, and we have a shared fate.

Barry Lopez

Barry Lopez, an author, essayist, and short story writer, is the recipient of the National Book Award, the Award in Literature from the American Academy of Arts and Letters, and other honors. His work includes *Arctic Dreams, Crow and Weasel, About This Life* and *Light Action in the Carribbean.*

Two Stories Becoming One

Kim Stafford

The divisions in my native state keep me awake at night.
We argue, we fight, we abuse and protect. We are an old
story of place, and a new story of change. Can these two
be one?

My wife has a friend who followed her graduation from the University of Oregon by suspending herself in trees in protest of imminent logging. Loggers would gather a hundred feet below her to shout, threaten, try to talk her down.

Given her training in the liberal arts, she found herself following these shouted conversations in all kinds of directions, usually resulting in mutual affirmations of life in Oregon, in the woods, in a common sense of home. One day, a logger heading back to town from falling trees asked her if he could bring her anything.

"I'd love a book," she shouted down to him.

"I'll bring you my favorite," he called back.

The next day, when she lowered a cord the hundred feet down to him, he tied on his book for her. She spent the day, suspended on her three-by-six-foot platform in the forest canopy, reading David James Duncan's *The River Why*.

This is one of many stories about our common ground.

I believe in the common story we are trying to live in Oregon. I believe in the conversation among us all, the search for the story of our future, which we will write together. We are many stories becoming one.

■

What is this place called Oregon? What principle gathers this place into one idea? It can't be weather, despite what strangers say. We are a land of rain and a land of sun. On the coast, expect rain. But out in Wallowa County they say, "We've got four seasons—every day." And it can't be the economy. We were timber; we were wheat. Now we are those, and many other things.

The principle of our Oregon identity is not weather, and it is not work. It is, instead, a contradiction. Our identity in the Oregon country consists of two stories that must be healed into one.

I find these two stories everywhere in our state, two versions of our character and our mission. These are the twin stories of the traveler coming to this place, and of the resident in this place. These two stories are at war in us. We must make peace between them.

In one story, we are a band of travelers newly arrived in the promised land. We come in a ship under sail, two centuries ago, with Robert Gray, viewing and naming the coast. We arrive in hatchet-carved canoes with Lewis and Clark, skidding off the mountains and hurtling down the great river of the western slope. We ride the undammed waters of the Lochsa, the Clearwater, the Snake and the Columbia. Like young salmon, we find the salt taste of the sea for the first time. We marvel at the gray and the green land, its rain and sun, its birds, its pure waters and its people: Klickitat, Chinook, Molalla, Clackamas. We write a long letter home, a report to our president, describing the place, its sparkling treasures, its dangers.

In this same story, we are a band of pioneers who follow a deepening rut of dust and mud across the continent. In our wagons we hold hives of bees. We hold our families. We hold apple saplings. We grip books of Genesis that explain our mission. We have guns and plows, axes and spinning wheels. We have pigs to root deep in the camas fields, to prepare them for wheat.

In this same story, this odyssey peopled with travelers, we are Woody Guthrie, come to this place for a month of creation in the Great Depression to write songs like "Pastures of Plenty" and "Roll On, Columbia." We are my own parents, Dorothy and Bill, arriving here indirectly from the Midwest by way of World War II. We are a band of refugees, boat people on their own kind of *Mayflower* from Vietnam, we are Old Believers, we are Finns, we are Palestinian, Hmong, Ethiopian, Russian Pentacostal. We have heard this is a safe and beautiful place, sometimes prosperous, sometimes welcoming. We are a story of arrival in hope.

This story is a young one. It has only been happening here for a couple centuries. It happens today. In this story, we arrive from California, refugees from a prosperity, a golden dream that went somehow askew. We hear there is a jade green dream to the north, and we seek it. We want to start over, and because we are new to Oregon, we make a few mistakes in our effort to live right. We donate a tithe to the Sierra Club, then cut the trees in our yard so we can have a clear view of the mountain.

We believe our wants are simple: a home, a job to do, a mountain to view and to visit. What else will we need in a place this fine?

The answer is this: We will need understanding. We will need to learn to care for the things we brag about.

We will need to know, and then to live, the second story of this place.

For there is this other story in Oregon: it is secondary, and it is older, and it is the future. It is a story that has been battered, assaulted, but will save us when we learn to tell it and to live it. This other story I do not know well. I am only forty-six.

It is the story of longer residence, of the Native way matured by more winters than there are bricks in Portland's Pioneer Square, more summers than there are sticky children at the Rose Parade. We glimpse this story sometimes, those of us who have come to the Oregon country to stay.

3   *Kim Stafford*

I glimpsed this one Sunday at the giveaway at Nespelem, when the dancing stopped, and a fancy dancer Native man stepped forward into the ring, holding up a bridle, calling out the name of a certain child. "To honor the passing on of traditional values," he said, "I would give to a certain grandmother and a certain granddaughter the gift of this bridle, which was my grandfather's, and a saddle which was my father's, and a mare that is mine, a young one, and fertile." He called the name of the granddaughter again and again, until she came out from the darkness, a young one, shy, maybe eight years old in her long skin dress and beads, came out from the shadows and took the bridle without a word, and disappeared.

In this story, this Native way, we do not live by the sale of commodities. We live by an exchange of gifts. We live by recognizing this place is giving gifts to us, every day, every moment of sun and clear rain, and we can only live here by giving to each other, and giving back to the land. That is how we heal the two stories: by giving and giving back.

We have to look each other in the eye and tell this story with care, for we live in a place where the two stories are at war.

In these two stories, two eras coexist, two ways of being. The two carry with them the desire to change the place, and the necessity of living with those changes for seven generations. A logger with his grumbling saw meets an old cedar.

A fisherman pulls an ancient Chinook from the river. A farmer harrows the camas prairie. A dam's turbine swallows the oldest river of our land. Someone young meets something old. The traveler meets the resident. Our prosperity is based on the meeting of these two stories, and we need to learn to carry out this meeting. If one story kills the other, we have nothing.

Carl Jung once made a prophecy about us. Americans, he said, will finally become Indians, natives of their place. If they don't, they will die and their place will die. He was talking about us, we who care about the place we live, who care about it beyond ourselves, we who gather in this work. And I want to ask us now, we who are both travelers and residents, how do our two stories get healed into one? How do we arrive, finally, in this place, and act simply in the matured character of the Oregon country?

I can only answer this question by telling a story, Lloyd's story. Lloyd Reynolds, the international citizen of Portland, spent his last days in pain, silent, unable to speak or to write, lying in his hospital bed inwardly composing a story in his mind to give to a child. He lay on his sheet, in each waking segment of his pain, putting together the particular telling of a story he wanted to give to a slow child named Christopher. Lloyd wanted to tell Christopher the story of St. Christopher, the strong monk boy who could do nothing right. That monk boy kept praising God in odd ways. He delighted in the seeds of dandelion, and sang as he scattered them in the garden of the monastery.

Finally, in Lloyd's telling, the exasperated abbot sent monk Christopher down to the river to wait and stay out of trouble. Christopher goes hulking down to the river and begins his vigil, and finally, after some days, he sees on the far bank a little child waiting to cross. Christopher strides into the water and easily wades the torrent, and he lifts the child to his shoulder to start back, but when they reach the deepest place, Christopher staggers. The child is heavier and heavier, crushing, and Christopher has to summon the deepest roots of his strength to carry the child to dry land, and set him down there. Then a light comes around them, and Christopher sees it is the holy child, who says to him, "You have been carrying all the grief of the world."

In the last hours of Lloyd's life, he summoned his own deepest strength, and managed to write that story down, and after his death it became a small book for the boy Christopher. They have this book at the Central Library in Portland, safe in the stacks, and the book ends with this thought: "We are all pilgrims traveling a path that frequently is filled with suffering. But if we share St. Christopher's loving helpfulness with each other, wild flowers will bloom along the way."

But this story doesn't end where Lloyd's life ended. It ends like this: On his last day at home, as his wife scurried to pack his suitcase for the hospital, Lloyd made his way outside to the garden, and there she found

Kim Stafford

him on his knees, with a spoon, awkwardly planting flower bulbs.

"Lloyd," she said, "you will never see these flowers bloom."

He smiled at her. "They are not for me," he said, "they are for you."

The salmon coming home? They are for you. The calls of wild geese? They are for you. The last old trees? They are for you and your children, to the seventh generation and beyond. They are all blooming into being for you.

When I was a visitor in Venice, my Italian friend Pino Zennaro, whose family has been in that city for 700 years, was showing me a series of drawings he had made as a young man. His drawings showed his love for the light, the water, the bridges and windows, the boats and the soft sunlight on his native place.

"Why," I asked him, "do you not do this art now?"

He looked at me. "When I was young," he said, "I would observe things, and make a drawing of them. I would do art on paper, and give it away. I liked that work very much, but it is not enough alone. Now, I am an architect. I restore the buildings of my city. Venice is the city of history, and the city of the future. There are old ways to do things here that will be the model for the new. We are making the future vision of how people can be together. My art is my city."

We can say this: My art is my city.

My art is Oregon. My art is the seventh generation. The problems of our time are political, economic and environmental, but their solutions are cultural. For the solution to war is not war; it is knowing other people as neighbors, as common citizens of earth. The solution to poverty is not wealth; it is learning true value.

The solution to environmental crisis is not scientific only; it is following the stories of our lives in this place to some convergence with the many lives sharing this place. Who will bring two stories into one?

Who will become native to this place? Who will plant the roots of color and plenty for another generation?

The true citizens of this place are those who say it this way: My art is the place I live and the people I live with. I have a job, but my art surrounds it, goes beyond. My art is my family, my tribe, my valley, my watershed: my long embrace of the Columbia's waters. Two stories? One life. This place says over and over, "My friend, I am not for me. I am for you."

Kim Stafford is a teacher, writer, and founding director of the Northwest Writing Institute at Lewis & Clark College. His most recent book is *The Muses Among Us: Eloquent Listening and Other Pleasures of the Writer's Craft* (University of Georgia Press, 2003).

This essay is adapted from a speech delivered to the Oregon Community Foundation on November 6, 1991. It appeared in the Winter 1996 issue of *Oregon Quarterly*.

Picking Fruit

Kathleen Holt

From lychee and waiwi to a valley of berries to a coconut in Portland.

1996

When he asks what sort of fruit he should pick up at the grocery store, I find myself reciting the same list: apples, oranges, bananas. Even in the middle of summer, when the produce section is ripe and burgeoning, looking its happiest and most colorful, my mouth forms shapes that make the same sounds: apples, oranges, bananas. Even if we buy a firm, fragrant cantaloupe or sweet seedless grapes, I often forget about them, and they go straight from the store to the fridge to the compost pile. After ten years on the mainland, I fear I am losing my imagination for fruit.

Some nights when I dream in color, I remember how well I once knew the names and flavors and smells and textures of Hawai'i. I knew the names of fruit, the flavors of them: crisp sweet mountain apples, tart guava, sour waiwi, succulent papaya. I knew the names and scents of flowers: hibiscus, plumeria, maile, ohia, ginger. I knew the mountains and the craters, the valleys and the rivers: Kohala, Hualalai, Puhimau, Hi'iaka, Waipi'o, Pololu, Wailuku, Kolekole. And all those shades of green of the landscape and blue of the water, so many that I couldn't begin to name them.

And I remember the sound of the place, of the trade winds and ocean waves always background music, of people speaking pidgin, a creole that combines words and phrases from several languages, with a sing-song cadence and telltale trilling and loping that make words run headlong into each other at breakneck speed, only to stop abruptly on a high note, as if every sentence spoken is a question. Say *moi moi* instead of sleep, say *bocha* instead of bathe. Say *hapai* instead of pregnant, say *ohana* instead of family. Drive *mauka*, toward the mountain, and then *makai*, toward the ocean, and you will find the place. Even if I try to work the words into conversation on the mainland, no one knows what I mean, and explaining sucks the melody from them.

1985

In a high school art class, we had to draw a bowl of fruit. I remember thinking, Well, this sucks—I can't draw. But I needed the class to graduate next year so I faked it. I drew a whole bunch of circles and ovals with some charcoal, not much effort at all. Then I titled it something like, "Fruit—Unpeeled" and explained to my teacher that I was deconstructing the form and shape of the fruit to display how fundamental it, and all of humankind, really was. I got an A.

I faked my way through most things back then. I wrote an essay about the Cold War metaphors in *The Catcher in the Rye* before even reading the book and ended up winning $50 in a county-wide writing contest. I invented a boyfriend who lived on another island and when the kids at school started doubting his existence and wanted proof, I killed him in a motorcycle accident. I walked around Kaiko'o Mall talking in a British accent, telling the clerks I was from Hong Kong. I pretended my family was a host family, that we weren't related, that I was staying with them until I could leave and go back to my other life, my better life, my not-so-Hawaiian life.

1988

Jeff has returned from Washington with Everclear, 190 proof and not for sale in Oregon. My University of Portland roommates and I are having a party and are making jungle juice to supplement the pony keg stowed in the basement.

"Watch," he says, pouring a scant amount into a pan and striking a match. The liquid bursts into a blue quivering flame. "Cool, huh?"

I try to hide my concern that we will be serving this highly flammable contraband to our guests, ladled out of a recently purchased blue plastic trash can, no less. We make gallons of the concoction with several containers of frozen orange juice concentrate, cut oranges and grapefruit, water, ice and Everclear. I'm not impressed with my first reluctant taste; it is merely orange juice with a kick to it.

Soon our chums and their chums, perhaps one hundred of them all told, arrive in giddy waves, washing through the small duplex looking for food and drink. We mingle and laugh and drink. We pass a Costco-sized bag of popcorn around the room. The jungle juice is a huge success, and soon the container is empty, except for saturated wedges of fruit, which we greedily grope for and suck dry. I am a new fan of the fruity concoction; my face is flushed red from the alcohol and the heat of the crowd.

Throughout the night, I have drunken conversations with young white people, many of whom I know from philosophy or theology or literature classes, so we try to talk about school, our common ground. Their voices still sound disappointingly flat and monotonous to my Hawaiian ear, like they speak a foreign language. The names of important people roll easily off their tongues: Nietzsche and Hesse, Camus and Goethe. In my haze, I try to grasp the sounds, to remember them so I can practice later when I'm alone and sober.

Soon our cobbled words fall into the basics of small talk: where, when, why. Many of them are from big West Coast cities: Portland, Los Angeles, Seattle, San Francisco. They think Hawai'i is a resort where everyone wears tacky floral print clothes and has flowers in their hair. They like to hear me talk, think the sing-song cadence of my words is charming. They ask if I can hula, if I can surf. They speak slowly so I can understand them and laugh with delight when I do.

It is an unremarkable scene of youth, but I can't help but feel lucky to be here, like I'm on the verge of something significant. Like wearing your first bra, like getting a pair of hand-me-down high-heeled shoes from your sister, like being invited to the adult table at Thanksgiving—that feeling of stepping forward into new skin, how you have to tug at it, wiggle into it, ease into it until it sort of fits. A little loose here, a little tight there. And if it's unbearable, you just keep trying new skins, and if you're lucky, you find one you can grow into.

1993

On our first road-trip together, Alex and I are stopped at the Oregon-California border by a lethargic, uniformed official of the U.S. Department of Agriculture, who asks dully, "Any fruit or vegetables in there?" We have a cooler full of drinks and snacks, among them an apple and orange or two, but I quickly and brightly say, "No," because I already know enough about Alex to know that he will either tell the truth or attempt to lie and fail miserably. The officer waves us through and in the silence that follows, that awkward silence between one person who has lied and the other person who knows, I say, "It's not like when you come from Hawai'i. Here, the fruit flies could just fly over the border if they wanted to." He looks at me with a surprise, laughs, and agrees that it seems like a stupid law. It occurs to me that eating the fruit before we cross the border is an option, but Alex and I have only known each other for a few months, and devouring fruit in silence on the side of a major highway seems like a terribly intimate thing to do.

1974–1977

Summer days picking fruit, a family excursion: We'd ride out along the Hamakua Coast with my mom and my grandparents looking for groves of trees, adults in the cab of the truck, my sister and I on wooden fruit crates in the bed. I was prone to car-sickness but the trips were short and being out in the fresh air seemed to help as well.

When he was alive, my Grandpa Maximo would come with us. He was the darkest man I'd ever seen, so the flashes of white on him were vivid: full head of hair, wide smile, palms that looked skinned. He was my grandmother's second husband, my mother's stepfather, and at that time, the only man in my life. He was born in the Philippines and had a thick Ilocano accent; his words rang like bells in my ears. We grandkids barely understood anything he said, but we loved him because he always seemed delighted with us. He always chuckled and mumbled something unintelligible but supportive-sounding before pressing a few dollar bills into our hands. The one time I understood an entire sentence he spoke, I watched his thick pink lips split apart in a blinding white smile before he said, "You could be like that Wonder Woman lady on TV when you grow up."

By the time I was nine, I could handle a ten-foot-long bamboo pole with a canvas bag on the end. The pole was thicker at the base and tapered up to the wire-rimmed bag at the top, like a fishing rod with a canvas sack at the end: Slip the bag around a dangling piece of fruit, catch the stem in the notch on the rim, tug and flick the pole lightly to break the fruit off the stem, catch it in the bag. Ten to twenty waiwi or lychee, a few guavas, or one or two ripe mangoes or lilikoi fit in the bag at one time. Palm over palm, I would bring the bag down to me, peering inside to see how I'd done. Waiwi, lilikoi and guava had perfect circles like belly buttons where they'd been plucked. Mango and lychee sometimes broke with a short piece of stem still attached like an umbilicus.

Waiwi, lilikoi and guava were too tart. I could drink them in juices but I never snuck bites of them while we were picking, just put them in the shallow fruit crates in the back of the truck. A full crate would get us a few bucks at Suisan Market later in the day. Mangoes were irresistible to all of us, even to my grandparents, who were like machines when they picked fruit. When one of us would hook that perfect one, we'd eat it then and there. I remember the fat ripe red ones, large and pulsing in my two small hands like a heart. How my crooked teeth would sink into the warm fruit, tearing hunk after hunk of the orange, inimitably sweet meat, the juice trickling down my neck, down inside the front of my grubby T-shirt, sticking to my chest and stomach.

My sister and I fought over the lychee. They didn't bring as much money as mangoes and were harder to find than guava, so we picked them because we loved them. They were small and hard-shelled with soft white meat inside, making them the fruit-equivalent of shellfish. I cracked through the tough shell with my dirty fingers to reveal the thin translucent layer containing the fruit juices like human skin contains blood. I pierced the layer with my teeth, biting through the firm succulent flesh until I hit the pit, which I sucked dry and spat at my sister. I've only found them canned in Asian-goods stores on the mainland, preserved in a syrupy sweet sauce of sugar and water, naked white, already stripped of their deep red shells. I refuse to even try them.

1997

Early in berry season, I'm the first one out in the new summer sun. I drive to the farms outside Eugene, approach the pleasant rural homesteads that advertise U-Pick produce, receive instructions and buckets and wander into the fields. Some years the crop ripens early enough to coincide with hay fever season, but I am undeterred. What a sight I must be —pale, sun-starved legs bent as I crouch awkwardly between short prickly rows of strawberries, straining for the fattest, juiciest ones that remind me of lychee. I sneeze often and blow my nose into a wad of Kleenex I retrieve from my shorts' pockets, a loud and long honk that breaks the country quiet and brings to mind Canada geese in the fall. I eat the ones I can't resist, the ones that go red as blood clear through and leave my lips and teeth stained the same color as my tissue-worn nose.

The valley is berry-crazy—strawberries, blackberries, blueberries, raspberries, huckleberries, salmonberries, thimbleberries, marionberries, gooseberries. Before our neighbor razed the wild, overgrown blackberry shrubs in his backyard, deer would come at dusk to feed and bed down. Now they travel to the slough in front of our house, where the bushes grow rampantly, and gorge themselves. We know this because when we search for ripe berries on evening walks, Alex must reach far into the highest branches to retrieve any fruit at all. My friend, a native Oregonian, spends all summer making berry foods—mixed berry jam, blackberry muffins, raspberries on vanilla ice cream sprinkled with Grape Nuts. She picks them wild on hikes, teaches me which are good to eat and which are poisonous. Even her dog whiles away summer days nimbly plucking blueberries in the backyard, until Heather chases her away and harvests them to share with us.

2001

After many years in Eugene, we live in Portland now. Alex has a job as a planning consultant, and every morning, puts on a tie and takes the bus to his office. I work at home, in the nook off the kitchen of our small rental house in Northeast Portland. I walk our dogs in the afternoon, when hours at the computer screen have made my eyes bleary and the crick in my right shoulder begins to ache. For the first few months, we carefully wandered the quiet neighborhood streets, finding our way by counting blocks—three blocks west, three blocks north, three blocks east, three blocks south. A perfect, manageable square.

Alex comes home one day with a brochure about produce gathered from organic farms throughout the West Coast and delivered to his office weekly. We pay $18.50 for a half order every other week. One of our first packages comes with mostly vegetables—salad mix, cabbage, carrots, broccoli, onions—but also with fruit: Encore mandarins, lemons, pineapple, oranges, Mutsu apples and a coconut.

Alex hefts the hairy brown orb in his hand, excited. "I've never cracked a coconut open before," he says. He shakes the fruit, cocking his ear to hear the liquid swish like a trapped ocean inside.

I've never cracked open a coconut either, but I don't admit it to him. I think he'll be disappointed in me, ask how I could be a coconut virgin when I was surrounded by palm trees in Hawai'i. Instead, I hold out my hand and he gives the fruit to me. It is an imperfect globe shaped more like a shelled filbert—or hazelnut, as everyone outside of Oregon calls them. It is palm-sized and has three eyeholes at one of the poles. It is rough with remainders of husk, unpleasant to the touch. On the trees, this fruit is so terribly protective of its soft meaty insides, covered first by the sinewy husk that breaks its long fall, then again by this nut-like shell. What is it hiding? What is it trying to keep secret?

"How do we do this?" I ask finally.

He seems neither disappointed nor surprised and looks through the material that has come with our bounty—a sheaf of paper with detailed information about each piece of produce and recipes graciously culled from cookbooks—and finds the instructions. With an awl and hammer, he pierces the three eyes of the shell; the first is easy, the next two harder. He turns the coconut upside down over a glass and pours out the liquid, which is thinner and clearer than I thought it would be. We each take a sip. "It tastes like coconut water," Alex says, shrugging. I nod.

He raises the hammer and swings it down onto the coconut with steady, concentrated blows. After four whacks, the shell begins to split and crack. With the fifth, the shell breaks into two hemispheres, east and west, along a jagged international dateline. We try to pry the thick meat from the shell with knives, but can only loosen tiny useless chunks. We nibble at the pieces. They are bland and chewy, only vaguely sweet.

"Should we break them into smaller pieces?" I ask, frustrated. My hands are sticky with the milk and dirty from the shell's brown residue.

"Okay," Alex says. He hands me the hammer and steps back.

I turn a half onto its flat side, bring the hammer down in a practice swing for aim, raise the hammer and bring it down again, making con-tact. The shell is softer than I imagined, has some spongy give to it. I raise the hammer higher and bring it down. Again. Again. Again. Soon, telltale cracks spread across the brown surface. I think briefly of Pangaea, of plate tectonics, of continents and their inevitable drift, then I bring the ham-mer down hard—perhaps harder than necessary—and the shell splits. Several smaller pieces scatter and skip across the countertop—into the sink, behind the toaster, onto the floor.

I pick up a fragment—a triangle about an inch long on each side that is flatter, has less arc and no hard-to-reach pocket where the meat clings fiercely and is difficult to retrieve. Newly confident, I pick up my knife and set to work, freeing the dense meat easily from their broken, manageable shells.

Kathleen Holt was assistant editor of *Oregon Quarterly* from January 1995 through June 2001. She is a freelance editor, graduate assistant in the English Department at Portland State University and editor of *Oregon Humanities,* the magazine of the Oregon Council for the Humanities.

This piece appeared in the Autumn 2001 issue of *Oregon Quarterly*.

Speaking Oregon

Brian Doyle

On the language that leads us home.

I spend a few days each month at a house on the coast, in the little village of Neskowin—"the place of many fish" in the Salish tongue once used there by the Tillamook people. The beach is open and alluring but I prefer to walk in the soft rolling hills that crowd along the shore like waves of earth. The hills are cut by old fire roads, logging roads, quarry trails, creeks named for panther and teal. Occasionally I find pathways made by deer that have pushed through the salal thickets like burly teenagers. In these hills are bears, bobcats, fishers. There is a rumor of cougar, that most graceful language of the remote woods.

Recently I tracked down a topographic map of my Neskowin hills and pinned it up in my office, under my window, which peers out over the river and into the West Hills—the Tualatin Mountains, as a friend of mine calls them. He is an Oregonian, 80 years old, an editor and writer and lumberman all his life. He is a fine man with a face like a piece of bark and a crewcut like a fresh-mown lawn. He came into my office the other day and stared at the map. "Hemlock in those hills, I bet," he said. "Some," I said. "Mostly second or third spruce." "Lot of alder in the cuts?" "Tons.

Salmonberry, too." "Thickets?" "Jungles." He eyed the map for a while and we talked some more about alder trees, which often curve together in canopies over streambeds. Alder of that sort dries crookedly, in the shape of its original bend; it is called tension alder and is the bane of sawmills, said my friend, who had wandered all through the Pacific Northwest as a lumberman's representative, visiting gyppo outfits and little mills and acquiring an astonishing knowledge of trees and bushes. Talk of alder led him to a discussion of ways to leach the red dye out of the wood, and that led him to a comparison of the tensile strength of hemlock and Douglas fir, and then to cottonwood, which makes the loveliest veneer for plywood. Cottonwood grows best near streams, and talk of streams led us to the water ouzel, or dipper, which lives on the edges of streams and feeds in them and sings like them. Dippers led to bears and elk and owls, all of which have slept in my friend's woods at Arch Cape. The owl, he said, was smoke-gray and the size of a child. We talked a while more and then he ambled off, his belly peering between his suspenders like a face between fenceposts.

A minute later I realized that he and I had been speaking Oregonian.

In 1964, when I was eight years old, I discovered that I lived on an island 33 miles wide and 133 miles long. The island had been called Paumanok for many centuries by the Shinnecock Indians who still live there. The discovery that I was a Paumanokan was my first taste of geography, and it was a great shock. I was *placed,* so to speak, for the first time; I was given a map much bigger than my boy-maps of yard, street, woods. I was also given a new language, a native tongue with words for the physical island (saltmarsh, kettlehole pond) and its creatures and places: scallops, bluefish, marsh hawks; Copaigue, Patchogue, Montauk.

A week later Sister Marie Aimeé told us that our island—unimaginatively rechristened Long Island by its seventeenth-century English and Dutch settlers—was part of a much larger state called New York. She also added that New York was one of *fifty* states. To prove this latter thesis she herded us into the school library to research the natural resources, crops, industries, arts, crafts, histories, literatures, populations and geologies of the United States, one state per child. She put fifty slips of paper in a hat and pulled them forth with a flourish, like tiny rabbits.

The boy in front of me got New York, and did a little touchdown dance at his luck; I was handed Oregon. I remember that the name seemed mysterious and ancient to me, brawny and muscular. A minute later we read the names of our states aloud, a litany of the Union, a poem of America chanted in the fluting voices of children. Oregon was ungainly in my mouth and fell out awkwardly: it opened softly and ended hard, like a love affair gone awry.

Many years passed. I moved from New York to Indiana to Illinois to Massachusetts. I learned more Oregon words: salmon, logger, river, cedar, fir. I learned names, too: Siletz, Trask, Tillamook, Prefontaine, Pendleton, Hazel Hall, Tom McCall. I never did learn the correct pronunciation of the state's name, though, and called it Ore-a-gone, like everyone else east of Idaho. So that was the name of the Oregon I did not know, a mythic place on the edge of the known world, as far away as I could imagine.

Then I fell in love with an Oregonian. We courted and married and moved to Oregon and had a daughter, an Oregonian. Now I live in the spacious word I could not say. It is the first word of a green language that is draped over the land like a spell. The land is older than the words and so there are places where there are no names. The hills and woods and high deserts poke through the language like mountains through mist. Its verbs are stories and its nouns are the threads of history by which we stitch ourselves to the places we want to call home.

I work on a high bluff over the Willamette River, at a university. The campus comprises some hundred acres. On those acres are trees beyond number, among them basswood, hornbeam, ironwood, madrone, mulberry, myrtle and redwood. In the oaks by the river there is a hawk's nest. It is a sharp-shinned hawk, I think, a fast hawk of the woods, a gray and dangerous hawk. Perhaps once a week I see the bird rocketing through the spangled oaks as if they were not there and he was slicing through fat air. He is a bird of the woodland, familiar with his trees, and I envy him that. I wish I knew the trees of my place as well as he knows his, and could slide among them like water.

Something about the hawk is Oregon to me. Perhaps it is his unerring sense of direction amid the thick trees. Perhaps it is his silence; I have never heard him utter a sound, and I think silence is a powerful word in the language of this landscape. Perhaps it is his sheer presence; there are more hawks in the West than there are in the East.

Three years ago I sat in my study in an ancient wooden house in Massachusetts, a house older than Oregon's statehood, and made a list of reasons to move. I had been offered a job editing a fine magazine in the city where my wife was born and raised. First reason to move: my wife wanted to go, and I love my wife more than I can tell you. Second reason: more hawks. Third reason: great state name, like Idaho or Montana, un-like Washington. Fourth reason: I wanted to go, to my great surprise. I loved Massachusetts, loved it with the abiding passion of an immigrant for the place he finds refuge, and I knew my little village by the sea, knew every inch of it, knew where nests and caves and broken boats were. Yet there was a part of me that inexplicably wanted to go West. Perhaps home and away are always at war. Perhaps adventure is a dream that curdles security. Perhaps Americans are indeed a people always leaning west.

"We all play at transporting ourselves new into new country, seeing freshly," writes William Kittredge, who was born in dry Oregon and who talks about storytelling as a means of living deeply, because he is con-vinced we can tell ourselves home, create stories that become homes and that home is the place where we are closest to recognizing what is sacred and how we fit into the sacred. By sacred I do not mean religion but spirituality, which has more to do with my elfin daughter asleep on my shoulder or with the dappled purple grapes that my old neighbor gives me every summer than it does with churches of any brand, although I have great affection for those quiet wooden places. Sometimes the way we fit into the sacred is through the door of a church but more often it has to do with the round shape of patience and grace under duress.

One of the ways that we see anew is to go to a new place; this is an ancient American urge, as old as the country, and there was some of that in my coming here. In a country that is not that old the Pacific Northwest is still the youngest place (except for Alaska, which is made of imagination and ice and which is still more a place to go to rather than a place to be). And in a young place there is more room for your story. I lived in Massachusetts for many years, and the stories of that ancient place are as thick as leaves on the ground, stories of great men and women and battles and ships, stories of love and hate and stone. Those stories fill the streets and libraries and rooms of the dusty old houses on the hills. The people of modern Massachusetts wander among old stories looking for space in which to sing new ones. There are those who need old stories to live by, who relish a thick past like a thick woods, as places rife with life, and I am such a man; yet I find in Oregon that I do not regret the loss of the old as much as I revel in the room to be new.

This surprises me, but I am in a new country now, where many things are surprising.

My wife was born here. My daughter was born here. My father-in-law is buried here, on a high hill under cedar and spruce trees. Like many Oregonians he was born elsewhere; like many Oregonians he thought this state was paradise, and he carved its earth with his hands and planted trees and flowers and his heart here. His greatest dream was to build his own home in the countryside. Near the end of his life he did just that, slicing through blackberry thickets with a machete and hammering fir and pine planks into a comfortable home on a creek, in the country town of Molalla. He and his three sons built that house. When he died his family sold the

Brian Doyle

home and lost some of themselves in the process. I think much of what he was is still there in his house. In fact I think he is there, in the crystal creek and cedar trees, in ways I cannot adequately explain.

My daughter was born in the fall. I carried her from the room in which she was born to another room. She was a prayer in my hands. I was sobbing, she was not. She lay awake for hours. I watched her for those hours, mumbling prayers and poems to her, staring at her newness. At some point she fell asleep. My wife was asleep, too. I went home to sleep, driving slowly past fields, firs, creeks, houses. Above my little girl there was a forest of stars: Pegasus, Cassiopeia, the Pleiades. The night was clear. The stars were swimming. I could not sleep and sat up thinking of my exhausted courageous wife and my new child, a new word in the world.

So I am woven into Oregon by the lines of my love. I test the lines; I think about living elsewhere, back in the birch woods of New England, perhaps; but then my daughter reaches for my hand and we wander through the grapes and blackberries and cedar trees behind our house and I revel in the lush language of this land.

It is my crewcut friend's native language and I am learning it from scratch. It has water and wood and wind in it. It has many dialects. Some are the speeches of creatures: Bear, Heron, Glacier, Fir. Some are the tongues of ancient peoples: Chinookan, Suislawan, Mollalan, Sahaptin, Waiilappuan, tongues once spoken all over the state, oceans of words now dried back to isolated ponds. Now there is Spanish, English, Japanese, Mixtec, cityslang. There are dialects of hate, there are stump stories and lovers' lies and the half-truths we tell each other called politics.

Where I live, in the slice of wet Oregon west of the Cascades, there are words and names made of mist layered like gray blankets. I am trying to learn them. I am fitting them in my mouth: the names of friends, fish, birds, plants, towns, hills, streets, the dead. Once I was a boy in a library with a word in my mouth and now I am a man in the mouth of the word. The word is beautiful and ungainly. It is a story. I am telling a little bit of it. My story is green and there is a fast hawk in it.

Brian Doyle is the editor of *Portland Magazine* at the University of Portland. He is the author of three collections of essays: *Credo, Saints Passionate & Peculiar* and, with his father Jim Doyle, *Two Voices*. His essays were included in *Best American Essays 1998* and *Best American Essays 1999*.

This essay appeared in the Spring 1994 issue of *Oregon Quarterly*.

A Rope in Rising Waters

Ross West

From the backrooms of the Smithsonian to mudflats near Bandon, Coquille Indians look for their past.

In April of 1995, just a week after spring rains had knocked the cherry blossoms from Washington, D.C.'s most famous trees, four Oregonians arrived in the capital. George Wasson, his niece Denni Mitchell, Jason Younker and his younger brother Shirod, all members of the Coquille Indian Tribe, were on an anthropological expedition to shed light on the early history of southwest Oregon. More profoundly, they were on a mission to preserve the history of a people—their own people—from the rising waters of time and fading memory.

To do so, they dug for shards of information in the millions of musty boxes buried deep within the Smithsonian Institution and other federal repositories. Week after week they pored over documents—most unread for generations, some decomposing in their hands—trying to gather the elements of a history whose narrative has been lost. All that remains is a tale told in fragments, gap-ridden and contradictory: journal entries, government records, maps, letters, treaties, tools, sketches and bones.

It will be up to future researchers to analyze the 30,000 pages of archival documents unearthed, copied and returned to Oregon. To some

will fall the task of assessing and interpreting individual documents—
dabs of paint in the portrait of a people—while others, as if viewing a
pointillist painting, will look for the interplay of all the dots together and
see in them a higher-level image.

The Coquille (ko-kwel´, not ko-keel´) Indians are one of about ten
major groups of native peoples on the Oregon Coast. No one knows how
large the tribe grew at its peak. Before contact with whites, before the
diseases, before the massacres, before the forced relocation. Today, fewer
than 700 Coquille remain.

George B. Wasson: *As I grew up it was disappointing to find that none of
the books on Indians had any information about my own tribe. I've always
known there wasn't much information on the Coquilles available here in
Oregon but that there was a lot of it in Washington, D.C.*

George B. Wasson is a Coquille elder with a long family history of
advocating for the tribe. In the process of earning a Ph.D. in anthropology at the University of Oregon, he guided the Southern Oregon Archival
Research Project from idea to reality, obtaining financial support from the
Smithsonian Institution, the Coquille Tribe and the University of Oregon.

Wasson got his first look at the riches housed in the capital in 1975
when he participated in the Smithsonian's American Indian Cultural
Resource Training Grant program at the Anthropological Archives of the
National Museum of Natural History. About that visit, he wrote,

> It was truly an overwhelming experience for me…. In my
> own naive way, I had no idea of the vast amount of informa-
> tion stored in those collections, and I had equally no idea of
> the even more vast amount of cultural items, artifacts, cer-
> emonial objects and even human (native) skeletal remains
> which had been collected over the past couple of centuries
> and stored away for either 'scientific' study, or just cultural

curiosity. At last I began to get a mental picture of the enormous material culture which had been swept away before the 'dying races' of America became extinct.

In the mornings, they would leave their rented apartments in Arlington, Virginia, and ride the sleek Metro railcars into the capital. Past the huge pillared edifice of the Smithsonian, through hallways with row after row of computer-laden offices, they would arrive at a quiet reading room, where faded words would transport them to an older world of horses, of cultures in collision, of atrocities.

Denni Mitchell: *We had an office in the back halls at the National Museum of Natural History Anthropological Archives. People don't usually get to go back there. You need to have a pass to get through security…. The reading room was small and cramped. The staff would bring us the materials we requested: old documents in boxes—musty brown pages, pages falling apart. Some documents were so fragile we had to wear gloves. We'd wear these white cotton gloves.*

Jason Younker: *We were small-town Oregonians in Washington, D.C., that was intimidating. Then the Smithsonian was so big, that was intimidating. Then reading about the massacres of our people. Concentrating all this in one time and one place with all of us in one room…at the end of the day, you were exhausted—mentally, physically, emotionally.*

Denni Mitchell: *We had such a short amount of time and we knew there was so much stuff there. If we saw something that pertained to our area we had to mark it to be copied. We couldn't sit and read it. This was hard. These things were so fascinating I just wanted to sit and read. Sometimes I couldn't help it, I had to read. There was my history, right there in my hands. Then one of the others would be saying, 'Hey, come on. You can't read that now.'*

Jason Younker: *[The staff] would bring boxes of papers separated into very general categories. You'd have to skim the pages to see if they had anything to do with this list we had of 600 key words. We had that list imprinted on our brains…. You'd wonder, 'What am I missing? Am I overlooking something?' You want more than anything to be thorough, but at the same time you're pressured to hurry. This is your once-in-a-lifetime shot to get the information together and bring it back for people who don't have that kind of opportunity.*

[The Oregon] students found a collection of place names for Coquille territory, which included explanations of the name origins; a map and census of the Coquille, made before their relocation to the Siletz Reservation in 1857; vocabulary lists; written accounts by settlers, Army personnel, missionaries, Indian agents and Indians; and a detailed unpublished map of a Coquille village in southwestern Oregon.
—*Research Reports,* the Smithsonian Institution

Jason Younker: *I found an entire folder dedicated to the Nasomah village massacre. I'd read about this in books, but to read something in a book is one thing, it is a whole different experience to hold the handwritten letter from the Superintendent of Indian Affairs explaining how the massacre happened.*

Miners flooded the area after the discovery of gold at Whiskey Run beach in 1853, and the town of Randolph sprang up over night. These miners quickly caused trouble with the local Indians. In November 1853, F. M. Smith, the local Indian Agent, wrote:

We are daily receiving accession to our population and many of those arriving are of the most reckless character, having no regard for law and order or life. I need the protecting arm of a military force to prevent outrages being committed upon the Indians by lawless whites.

No military help was forthcoming, however. On January 28, 1854, three lower Coquille villages were burned down by a party of miners led by George H. Abbott, William Packwood and A. F. Soapy. The village structures were set afire before dawn while the inhabitants slept inside, and those attempting to escape were gunned down. At least sixteen men, women and children were killed. When Smith objected to these proceedings, the miners threatened to 'tie [him] to a tree and whip him like a dog.' Smith, the only government official in Coos County at the time, quickly resigned.

—Mark Tveskov

Mark Tveskov's UO doctoral thesis in anthropology will focus on the period of contact (1800 to 1900) between settlers and Indians of the southern Northwest coast. Tveskov, experienced archival researcher and UO anthropology doctoral candidate Dennis Griffin and UO undergraduate Jeff Weidemen each went east for one week to join the research activities.

Jason Younker: *All our lives we were not taught our heritage. Then to go back there and look at how our ancestors were treated by the government, the pioneers . . . it was very emotional, very hard to deal with. Having the personal connection to the people that were slaughtered made it all the more difficult. How could people treat other people like that? When you read these things, it's easy to relate to the Jewish Holocaust.*

Luther Cressman founded the University of Oregon's anthropology department in 1935. An Episcopal minister who was married for a time to Margaret Mead, Cressman doggedly pursued his career for more than forty

Ross West

years, establishing himself as the preeminent Northwest anthropologist.

In 1953 Cressman had written, "Four or five years more work should be devoted to this problem of Oregon Coast prehistory in order to formulate the various stages of development...before the sites are destroyed." Forty years later we find ourselves asking many of the same questions and contending with the same natural and human forces threatening coastal archaeological sites."

—Madonna Moss, in "Luther Cressman and the Coastal Prehistory Program"

Two anthropologists have spurred UO efforts to help the Coquille Tribe to discover, understand, interpret and manage its past. Soon after joining the UO faculty in 1990, Jon Erlandson and Madonna Moss—husband and wife—grew interested in the Coquille. Since that time they and a number of their students have been at the center of a flurry of Coquille research: identifying, studying and excavating a variety of archaeological sites; providing classroom and field training in archaeology to Coquille tribal members; working with the tribe to develop a comprehensive cultural resources protection plan; and advising Coquille students Wasson, Mitchell and Jason Younker (Shirod Younker is an undergraduate at Oregon State).

Jason Younker: *Three of us from one tribe—from a small tribe—working toward graduate degrees, that's unheard of.*

Last winter and spring, Jon Erlandson, Mark Tveskov and Jason Younker began analyzing objects gathered by Luther Cressman at a Coquille village site in the early 1950s.

George B. Wasson: *Artifacts and reality are different. [Scientists] can uncover rocks and bones and sticks. The danger is that these things will be focused on. The reality of culture is in the spoken word. Until you can find valid ways to connect these objects with a spiritual view you have only part of the story.*

"There has always been in anthropology an interest in 'the other,' but as times have changed and the ethnic makeup of anthropology classrooms has changed, the definition of 'the other' has also changed. Go back 100 years or even 50 years in anthropology and you will find some amazingly demeaning interpretations of native peoples. But today, there is a growing understanding that we need to leave behind the discipline's colonial past. We're on the forefront of a more inclusive type of anthropology. By training native scholars we are contributing to a more diverse view of the past."

—Jon Erlandson

George B. Wasson: *One of the more exciting results of my experiences with the science of the university is how it supports ethnographic information. Some of the oldest legends speak of tribal experience with tsunamis, earthquakes, volcanic eruptions, one even tells of the first arrival of salmon to the coastal streams. Now I can relate the scientific account of prehistory with traditional mythology.*

Jason Younker: *I'm planning to become a professor at the university level. There are not many American Indian faculty members at American universities. I will provide a unique perspective.*

The group of around twenty, a mix of university people and Coquilles, had been gathering all morning at the mud flats near Bandon, arriving in different cars, pulling on their rubber boots, toting equipment to be used in the excavation. Then they gathered together in a circle. A stalk of sage was lit, its gray smoke hovering in the air, mingling with the smell of sea and mud, sanctifying the day's work. Someone said a prayer.

Later on, an archaeologist working near Denni Mitchell said, "Denni, look." He pointed toward something half-buried in the mud—some cedar stakes and, between them, woven roots. The construction had once been part of an elaborate weir system the Coquille used for centuries to trap fish.

Denni Mitchell: *Then we found another. It was straight and even in its stitching. The spacing between the sticks and the twining was perfect. Hundreds of years in the mud and it was absolutely gorgeous. I started thinking about my ancestors, who had been right there where I was standing—who they were, what they thought about, how they lived. And what happened between then and now.*

Denni Mitchell: *It is my obligation and my responsibility to share what I can learn with the rest of the tribe. I do this with my own kids and the kids in the tribe. The kids especially need to know.*

Jason Younker: *We are providing nothing less than a cultural foundation for the youth of the Coquille.*

Denni Mitchell: *Some of those baskets from the weir are still out there buried in the mud and gradually getting washed away by the current.*

The past is prologue.
—National Archives motto

George B. Wasson: *There was no grand plan, no road maps or formulae for young Indians to follow in finding themselves in the big picture of the American Indian cultural-historical milieu. Each tribe or nation was in a different situation; in a different boat adrift without adequate knowledge of navigation or with no obvious means of propulsion.*

It seemed as though the ancient Flood Myth of the Coos Bay area was being played out again, wherein the People who had rushed to their canoes in advance of the rising waters were set adrift, except for those who had prepared by stashing long ropes in their canoes. They could tie up to the tops of the tall fir trees protruding from the mountain tops and gradually let themselves back down as the waters receded. While those with shorter ropes were either capsized or forced to cut loose, others with no ropes at all were swept far away into another land.

Ross West is assistant director of the University of Oregon Office of Media Relations. His work has appeared in *ICON Thoughtstyle, Orion, Oregon Heritage* and other publications. He was the text editor for the *Atlas of Oregon.*

This piece appeared in the Winter 1996 issue of *Oregon Quarterly.*

A Circle of Words

Beth Hege Piatote

Two families honor the words of their ancestors
with an exchange of gifts in the Wallowas.

On the morning of July 27, 1997, two families gathered separately near Wallowa Lake, Oregon, ready to make an exchange that would put to rest a century-old regret. The sky was alternately bright and cloudy as one group, led by Keith Soy Redthunder, a member of the Chief Joseph band of Nez Perce, gathered on a grassy knoll beside the lake, praying and singing songs of the ancient Seven Drum religion. The other clan, the Wood family, descendants of C.E.S. Wood, waited at a public park to be summoned by the Nez Perce. At least forty people—including family and friends—met at each location. There, on that morning, they waited and prepared to complete a conversation that began between two men, their ancestors, more than 100 years ago.

The story of these two families coming together starts long ago, under tragic circumstances. The year was 1877. The Nez Perce people were being forcibly removed from their homeland in northeastern Oregon, and the U.S. government declared war on them. In a flight that lasted four months, Chief Joseph of the Wallowa band of Nez Perce led 750 of his people—including women and children, the elderly and the ailing—over 1,500 miles of mountainous terrain from Oregon to Montana in an effort to find refuge in Canada. Although the Nez Perce people were brilliant in evading the military, these clans of families were overmatched by a force of 2,000 young male soldiers. The war came to an end at the Bear Paw Mountains, just thirty miles south of the Canadian border, following five days of fighting in bitterly cold weather and snow in October 1877.

According to the best-known account of the Nez Perce surrender, Chief Joseph rode from his camp with five Nez Perce warriors to General O.O. Howard's camp and offered his rifle. His surrender speech, offered through an interpreter earlier that day, was recorded as follows:

> Tell General Howard I know his heart. What he told me before, I have it in my heart. I am tired of fighting. Our chiefs are killed. Looking Glass is dead. Toohoolhoolzote is dead. The old men are all dead. It is the young men who say, yes or no. He who led the young men [Ollokot] is dead. It is cold, and we have no blankets. The little children are freezing to death. My people, some of them, have run away to the hills, and have no blankets, no food. No one knows where they are—perhaps freezing to death. I want to have time to look for my children, and see how many of them I can find. Maybe I shall find them among the dead. Hear me, my chiefs! My heart is sick and sad. From where the sun now stands I will fight no more forever.

The man who recorded those words, Lieutenant C.E.S. Wood, was General Howard's aide-de-camp. On that day, Chief Joseph and Lieutenant Wood beheld each other in a moment heavy with tragedy and grief, in a situation that made an alliance impossible.

Yet these two men would someday become friends, and one day, long after they both were dead, their descendants would face each other again.

Although C.E.S. Wood performed his obligations to the U.S. Army, he believed that the war against the Nez Perce was "morally reprehensible and unjust," according to his great-granddaughter, Mary Wood, a professor at the University of Oregon School of Law. In 1884, C.E.S. resigned from the military and became a lawyer in Portland, and he advocated on behalf of the survivors of Joseph's band.

Following the surrender, some of Joseph's band, those of the Whitebird clan, fled to Canada. The others were sent to a prison camp in Leavenworth, Kansas, and later to Oklahoma, where many of them died. They were all cast into a diaspora: Chief Joseph and his people became exiles, forbidden by the U.S. government to return to their homeland of the Wallowas.

Chief Joseph himself traveled several times to Washington, D.C., to fight for his people's return to Oregon, but government agents argued that the hostility of the white settlers was too severe to allow it. Eventually, however, the Nez Perce returned to the Northwest. In the years of 1884 and 1885, the survivors who were agreeable to Christianity were sent to live on the Nez Perce reservation around Lapwai, Idaho. The others, including Chief Joseph, were sent to the Colville reservation in eastern Washington.

It was during these years that C.E.S. Wood developed a relationship of mutual respect and friendship with Chief Joseph. In 1889, Wood asked Joseph for permission to send his son to visit Joseph on the reservation. Chief Joseph agreed, and in 1892, thirteen-year-old Erskine Wood spent the summer living with Chief Joseph; the next year, young Erskine returned to spend another season with Joseph's family.

Erskine Wood, like his father, was a writer and kept diaries of his days at Nespelem living in Chief Joseph's tipi. He published one of the diaries at the age of ninety, and it included this recollection of Chief Joseph:

> He was the kindest of fathers to me, looking after me, providing
> for me, caring for me, and, it must be said, sometimes gently

rebuking me when necessary. His wives made my moccasins, and Joseph, himself, made me a bonnet out of muskrat fur, with a big eagle feather standing upright, and little red medallions cut out of blanket sewed against the fur.

In an interview with the Wenatchee (Washington) *Daily World* in 1956, Wood said that Joseph "took me into his teepee and into his heart and treated me as a son. . . . We ate together, hunted deer together, and slept together. I can say truthfully, knowing him was the high spot of my entire life."

His children and grandchildren were particularly well acquainted with Erskine's stories of living with Chief Joseph, as he recounted the stories often and always with fondness, says Mary Wood.

■

But along with those happy memories was also a sad one: a deep regret. "It happened at the end of the second season he lived with Joseph, when he was saying good-bye," Mary Wood says. "C.E.S. asked Erskine to ask Joseph if there was a gift he could offer in recognition of the admiration he felt for Joseph, and in return for the hospitality that he had extended to young Erskine. Joseph replied that he would like a fine stallion to improve his herd, but Erskine never conveyed that message back to his father. He looked upon Joseph as such a great man. He thought he deserved much more than a horse and thought it was too small of a request. As a young boy, he lacked judgment."

Wood says that her grandfather lived to be 104 years old, and that in his later years, he repeatedly spoke of this regret.

"We knew about the regret for years, but we didn't know that anyone else knew," Wood says. "It turned out a lot of people knew about it outside of our family. A funny thing happened: The story appeared on Ken Burns's documentary series, 'The West'.... I didn't even watch that episode, but people called me the next day saying, 'Your family's story was the capstone of this documentary.' I went back and watched it, and sure enough it was. Our family had been talking about giving a horse as a symbolic gesture for years, but we didn't know how to go about it. This film really served as a catalyst. It was a sign that the time was right."

Wood began to speak with her family about redressing the regret. At the same time, her aunt, Katherine Livingston, who learned of Erskine's regret for the first time by watching the Burns documentary, had also started a fundraising effort within the family. Soon the various branches of the Wood family came together—nearly sixty members and a dozen of their friends—to raise the money to buy a young Appaloosa stallion.

Horseman Rudy Shebala says he read Erskine Wood's diary and knew about Chief Joseph's desire to improve his herd of horses. It was one of many inspirations he felt as he and others developed an Appaloosa breeding and training program on the Nez Perce reservation in Idaho in 1994.

Shebala, director of the Young Horseman Project for the tribe, has seen the project grow to eighty horses and employ at least twenty young people each year. The program has developed a new breed of Appaloosa, using a Turkish strain of stallions. "Historically, the Nez Perce people had the ability to selectively breed horses, and we thought we could do it again," he says. "We wanted to create a strain of horse that would again be unique to the Nez Perce."

Shebala says the return of horses through this program has strengthened the Nez Perce culture and economy. "It has brought people back to things they haven't used in a long time," he says. "People have begun to sing songs that were obsolete without the horses. They're bringing out their trappings and doing beadwork and making saddles again.

"We've taken our horses back to battlegrounds where our people were lost, and we do memorials to remember them. We do a pipe ceremony and an empty saddle ceremony, with the horses dressed for a man's horse and a woman's horse. The horse is so visual. It is a powerful memory of how our people were scattered to see the empty saddles," he says. "The horses have a sense…they sense their place in the ceremony."

Shebala says a lot of people are interested in the horse program, so it doesn't surprise him when someone stops by to visit. One day, he says, a woman came by and asked some questions. "I was showing her around and talking about the program," he says. "Then I started telling her about Erskine Wood, and you know what? That lady I was talking to said she's his granddaughter."

■

During the spring and early summer, Mary Wood and her eighty-six-year-old father, also named Erskine Wood, and her twin sister, Becky Wood Hardesty, made several trips to Nez Perce country—the Colville reservation, the Nez Perce reservation in Lapwai (where Mary Wood met Shebala), the Umatilla reservation in northeast Oregon, and the Wallowas—to work out the details of presenting the gift. It was important to find the proper recipients of the gift and arrange for the proper cultural ceremony.

"It was very clear who should receive the horse, because everyone we talked to gave the same answer," Wood says. "Even though the Nez Perce tribe is located in Lapwai, everyone realized the gift was offered in Nespelem [Washington] and that we should find the closest living descendant on the Colville reservation. That person is [Keith] Soy Redthunder.

"I asked Horace Axtell [a Nez Perce elder at Lapwai] how to go about approaching Soy Redthunder about this gift, because I wanted to make it clear that it wasn't a gift from one person to another but a gift to a whole family from another family. He said, 'This is how you say it: We would like to give a stallion in trust for the words spoken 100 years ago.' And I thought that was a beautiful and elegant way of saying it. Soy immediately grasped the significance of that," she says, "and things went on from there."

Soy Redthunder, for his part, was surprised the first time the Wood family contacted him last spring.

"I couldn't believe it was happening," Redthunder says. "I didn't know exactly how to take it. I think Indian people are always skeptical at first. I don't think Indian people can look back and say the White Man's word was worth anything. A word spoken ten years ago is likely forgotten. So to hold someone's word for 104 years and still fulfill it—well, just think of all the promises that were broken just during that time," he says. "I needed to meet the family and ask a few questions, and when I did, I was very pleased with their answers."

He extended an invitation to the Wood family to participate in the spring root ceremony at the Colville reservation in April 1997. "There always has to be preparation to receive a gift," Redthunder says. "When they came to us, they were not treated as strangers. When they came to our Longhouse, people didn't spurn them. They were honest people, and you could recognize that right away. There was never any question that they were sincere."

Mary Wood says that she and her sister, Becky, were moved by their experiences at the root ceremony, where they ate camas, wild potato, bitterroot, koush, and other roots. "It was symbolic and important to us, because our grandfather had lived in Joseph's tipi, and his wives had gathered roots for him, and he had his particular favorites. So for us to go back 100 years later and eat these roots was really an amazing experience," Wood says. "One of the elders who served us the roots said, 'Here, this is what your grandfather liked.' We didn't know, but she knew. She remembered from a visit he made to the reservation [as an adult]."

In June, Mary Wood returned to Colville to meet with Redthunder and make the final selection of a horse. Wood had sorted through the pedigrees and papers of some 500 Appaloosa stallions and narrowed the choices down to a dozen. She presented the papers on the twelve horses, as well as videotapes, to Redthunder and other horse experts on the reservation. Together they chose a classic black-and-white stallion named Zip's Wild Man from a breeder in Utah.

During that meeting, Wood suggested they plan the ceremony, which the two families had agreed to hold in the Wallowa Valley in honor and recognition of Chief Joseph's homeland. The Woods had invited N. Scott Momaday, a Pulitzer Prize-winning Kiowa writer, to speak at the ceremony about the importance of horses in Native American culture. It was Momaday who, in his rich and powerful voice, had narrated their story on the documentary series that had nudged them to action so many months earlier.

But Redthunder said no, there would be no plan for the ceremony.

"I said I think everything must come from the heart. You can't script emotion. You can't choreograph honesty. It has to come from the heart. And that's how we did it," he says. "Everything went according to no plan."

Sunday morning, July 27: The descendants of Chief Joseph and C.E.S. Wood were about to face each other, in a moment not of tragedy but of happiness. The timing was fitting. Just a few weeks earlier not far from where they gathered, a ceremony had marked the return of the Nez Perce to the Wallowas after 120 years, as landowners and managers of a 10,300-acre wildlife preserve. The land was acquired with funds the Bonneville Power Administration paid the Nez Perce as compensation for building four dams along the Snake River.

As the Wood family waited at the park, Horace Axtell led a ceremony among the Nez Perce people in a private setting beside the lake. "It was a time to prepare so the words would come out with good feeling, like a blessing for what would take place that day," Axtell says. "The women, men, and children who came, they were all there to witness this blessing."

When the preparations were complete, the Wood family joined the Nez Perce, bringing the horse with them. "They sent someone to bring us up. We didn't know where we were going until we got there," Mary Wood says. "When we arrived, we saw that all branches of the Nez Perce were represented: from Colville, Lapwai, Umatilla, and from Whitebird's clan in Canada."

Soy Redthunder began the ceremony with a prayer, then offered gifts to the Wood family. He called Mary and her father, Erskine, forward and gave them beautiful woven blankets. The one he offered Erskine had the words "I will fight no more forever" in the design—the words of Chief Joseph as recorded by C.E.S. Wood in 1877.

The Wood family then offered their gift—a fine stallion, just as Joseph had requested. "Dad [Erskine Wood] called out the stallion, and it was very spirited," Mary Wood recalls. "It started to rear up on its hind legs. It was a beautiful sight. Soy asked Tommy Waters [a Nez Perce from Colville] to take the stallion for him, and the stallion quieted instantly. The Nez Perce sang a sacred song written for that occasion, and it was beautiful."

Momaday spoke, and other people offered words. As the ceremony ended, both families formed receiving lines and greeted each other. Mary Wood, at the request of Soy Redthunder, had written a small booklet to record the story of the gift, which was distributed to everyone there.

Axtell describes the event as a deeply gratifying exchange between two groups of people. "It was a great feeling, especially when the beautiful horse was introduced," he says. "In our time we had a lot of these beautiful horses, and now they can revive and grow among our people again. It was touching to my heart to see this with my own eyes, and to hear the words spoken by the Wood family and the Nez Perce people."

After the ceremony, the Redthunder family took the stallion back to the Colville reservation. They are planning to breed the horse and possibly start an Appaloosa program on the reservation. Redthunder says that the horse is a great symbol to the Nez Perce people. "Treaties written down were never fulfilled," he said. "Yet this one family can turn around and fulfill spoken words between two people more than 100 years old. To make those words good now is an extraordinary thing."

Wood says that for her family, to "complete a circle of words" brought a sense of calm as they put to rest a regret of someone they all loved. "It's amazing to me that I felt this endeavor of ours was motivated by sadness, as if the regret had been passed down in our family. But not long after we got started, the sadness was transformed into incredible joy. By the end of it, I felt that this horse was not meant to be given 100 years ago. It was a gift that our ancestors left us, to have the opportunity a century later to renew this relationship. It was their gift to us."

Beth Hege Piatote is a writer and Ph.D. candidate in Modern Thought and Literature at Stanford University. She is Nez Perce enrolled at Colville and is currently working on a collection of short stories.

This essay appeared in the Spring 1998 issue of *Oregon Quarterly*.

Another 100 Years

Ian McCluskey

*Saying goodbye to the family ranch and, with it,
a way of life.*

When I was young, I hid in the barn. My dad stacked the bales like bricks, making tunnels and trapdoors; I'd crawl through them, straw stabbing my palms, seeds trickling into my ears and socks. My mom spent her summers here, growing up. Her grandfather bought her a horse, said a kid shouldn't grow up without a horse. My sister and I would lope across the pasture, bareback. I wish he'd seen us ride. Half the barn collapsed a few years ago. Rain rusted the tin roof orange. I walk here, now, scan the dust for hoof-prints.

When we visited, my sister and I would sleep in the living room. I snuggled under the weight of Grandpa's Coleman sleeping bags. They had pictures of fishermen, rods arced, steelhead leaping, frozen in the moment of the catch. I'd flip through old Sears catalogues and make Christmas lists, believing spiked boots and saddles—even the catalogues themselves—would never be discontinued. The fire hissed and popped, as the clock chopped off another hour. Beyond the steamed windows, logging trucks grumbled as they passed, trailing a wake of mist and mud.

My great-grandmother would stand in the kitchen, peeling apples, humming hymns.

Grandma was a compact woman, elbow-high to just about anyone. When my great-grandfather built the "new" ranch house in 1956, he made the cabinets the perfect height for her. She'd scramble eggs and flip bacon, each morning at sunrise, while Grandpa hiked across the fields to pitch hay for the cattle.

On the living room mantel was a photo of him, raking hay in front of the barn. It is sunny and he's stripped down to his undershirt. His brown pants, worn shapeless with work, are held by suspenders. Years later, I found the suspenders hanging on a nail in the garage. I'd wear his boots every time I returned to our ranch; they fit as if I had ordered them myself from the cobbler. I never met my great-grandfather, though. He died the year before I was born.

My mother once snapped a photo of me dressed in Grandpa's wool shirt and those suspenders, wearing his steel hard hat and clutching his felling ax. The trunk of a cedar fills the background. When I showed my great-grandmother the photo, she said, "Oh, yes, that's Walt at the summer camp." No, Grandma, I told her, that's me. But when I look into the image, at the sunlight filtering silver and gray through overhead branches, blending with the plaid of the shirt, glinting on the ax blade and hard hat, shadowing my face, I'm not so sure. Grandpa was the only left-handed member of the family, besides me. When he wasn't on a summer logging crew, he taught school. Similarly, I taught for several years and spent summers earning wages on ranches.

I'd return to the ranch on holidays and the gaps between semesters and summer jobs. I'd stand in the living room, holding a Stetson in my hands. Breaking horses had bowed my legs and squared my shoulders. Grandma would be on her couch, wrapped in a crocheted shawl and propped by pillows. "You look more handsome than ever," she'd say, but I think she really meant that I looked more and more like Grandpa.

Twenty-five years after Grandpa collapsed from a heart attack, Grandma still woke up early, shuffled into the kitchen and made breakfast. We'd sit, my family and me, at the Formica table trimmed in chrome, watching the dew melt off the grass. The tap water, as always, flowed from the spring, cold, mossy, delicious.

The last Thanksgiving with Grandma, I helped her sugar strawberries from the garden so they could be jarred and frozen. Autumns we made ready for spring; spring we made ready for autumn. I wanted to believe, as I stood beside Grandma carving the stems from the berries, staining our hands, that our tasks were enough to keep everything going.

That year, spring came as it does: The rain tapered and the pastures steamed, and the creek beyond the barn swelled. Apples blossomed. We laid Grandma in a plot beside her husband, a few paces from other graves with our family names. I wore Grandpa's Stetson. We sang "Amazing Grace."

The relatives loaded their cars, then drove away.

Six generations of our family grew up here, but after Grandma died, a lawyer placed the ranch in a trust. I don't know what that means, but I know we can't pay the inheritance taxes. So we left the ranch. We left the harrow wedged in the field, left the piles of horseshoes and drawers stuffed with pocket knives and padlock keys. We left the boxes of nails pulled and bent back into shape.

Now, my last visit, I take down the Coleman bags. The fisherman still bends his rod, the steelhead keep leaping. I tug on Grandpa's boots, hike across the field to the barn, pants swishing through wet grass, socks bunched at ankles. Rain rolls from the mountains, pastures steam, apples bloom. I wish it could be as simple—to dust the Mason jars in the cellar, to oil the tractor, to stretch the barbwire again—as if the momentum of seasons and our devotion to tasks could carry us another hundred years.

Ian McCluskey

Ian McCluskey lives in Portland. He is at work on a collection of essays about Western traditions that have survived into the twenty-first century.

This essay appeared in the Autumn 2000 issue of *Oregon Quarterly*.

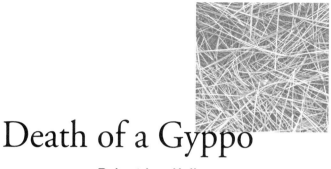

Death of a Gyppo

Robert Leo Heilman

*Anyone with a 'dozer and a chainsaw and a little luck
could set up and make a living—maybe even a fortune.*

The look and feel of the wood got to me. Funny how that works, how a rough-sawn pecky cedar one-by-twelve in your hands can conjure up memories, put you for a moment right back where you were fifteen years and more ago. I paused for a moment, holding the board but awash in the ghost smells of sawdust, gasoline, motor oil, rusting iron and damp cotton Lone Star work gloves. My sixteen-year-old son and my nephew, eighteen, stood looking at me.

"This here's some historical wood," I told them. The boys looked puzzled. It was just a pile of old wood to them—a mess they'd rather not be cleaning up. The pile of gray boards lay on the ground, my pickup truck backed up to it. Why this pause, this staring at an old board?

"This is Clason lumber," I tried to explain, "You know Jim Clason. Well, me and his grandpa, ol' Stewart, used to cut this stuff." Stewart Clason was the first logger in the South Umpqua to hire me when I arrived from Los Angeles without a clue as to what it meant to work in the woods.

We were in my friend Brian's back yard, over in Tortilla Flats, a Farm Home Administration low-income housing tract that didn't exist back when Brian and I first went to work for the Old Man. The fence posts had finally rotted and the fence had blown down, lain there all summer and now it was September, time to haul it off before the rains came and the wood got too wet for kindling and the ground too damp to drive across the lawn.

"Damn, that was a long time ago," I added, hoping they'd maybe understand a little of what it meant to be handling wood that had been logged and hauled and milled by a gyppo operator who'd died in the woods back before these two boys reached puberty. If they understood, it was only a very little and there wasn't much use in trying to explain it.

"Well, what the hell you guys waiting for? You stand around spacing out, making me wait. Come on, let's get this show rolling—dime holding up a dollar, boys." I tossed the board into the back of the truck. "Stack 'em neat now."

Gyppo isn't a word you'll find in most dictionaries, nor one you hear often in cities. Like many colloquialisms, it started out as a bit of derisive slang, meaning a logging or mill boss who was likely to "gyp" his employees and creditors—someone who functioned on a shoestring budget, a fly-by-night operator, a gypsy. Over the years though, the connotation has shifted from the instability and unreliability of small-time operators to the virtues a gyppo needs in order to survive—courage, self-reliance, common sense, hard work, the ability to improvise and an almost pathological optimism.

The woods were once filled with these wily independents, each as "various-minded" and "ready at need" as Odysseus in a hard hat. In the years immediately after World War II, gyppos were the rule in Southern Oregon rather than the exception. Demand for wood was high and the equipment wasn't expensive. Anyone with a 'dozer and a chainsaw or a portable mill and a little luck could set up and make a living—maybe even a fortune.

It was, by all accounts, a too-brief golden age, cut short by periodic housing slumps and a technological productivity "arms race." The big outfits drove their undercapitalized competitors out of business by harvesting ever larger amounts of timber increasingly faster and cheaper with increasingly sophisticated (and increasingly expensive) equipment.

The title has grown respectable in direct proportion to the increasing rarity of genuine gyppos. I've heard men with scores of employees and millions of dollars invested in yarders, bulldozers and trucks proudly describe themselves as humble gyppos. Most of them are the sons or grandsons of gyppos, men who've inherited some of the traditional mindset though not the precarious existence. Certainly, none of them would trade their sweetheart corporate deals and well-financed shows for the old man's hardscrabble assets.

Working for Stewart was, I realize now, very much like working in a living history museum. Everything he had was obsolete and either built by his own hands out of old scraps and pieces of discarded equipment or modified almost beyond recognition. His bulldozer, a little gasoline-engined 1931 McCormick–Deering, had a hand-crank starter that required two men to turn it over on cold mornings and only one if the weather was warm. A 1940 Dodge deuce-and-a-half-ton truck with a homemade "A" frame boom served as his yarder, skidder and log loader. A relatively modern 1958 Ford flatbed truck with bunks cobbled from scrap steel hauled the necessarily short logs to the mill.

The heart of S.R. Clason Lumber Company was his mill, one of those old circular-saw-and-carriage contraptions of the sort that turn-of-the-century melodrama villains were fond of tying hapless maidens to. Driven by a quirky art-deco Case industrial engine and an improbable arrangement of belts, pulleys and chains, it wasted an incredible amount of wood.

With its too-wide saw kerf, he lost a one-inch board in sawdust for every three rough-cut boards it produced. The wonder was that we produced any lumber at all.

Breaking down was more than just likely—it was a way of life. An efficiency expert hired to analyze S.R. Clason Lumber Company would have tossed away his time/motion study clipboard by lunch on a typical day. In such a case, the Old Man would have offered him a cup of coffee from his thermos and said with a grin, "You know, I believe you're right, son. It can't be done. Why, if a man had any sense he'd give it all up and get him a real job. But then, I never had much sense."

Actually, there was a certain method to his madness. In theory, at least, what he lost in efficiency was made up by what's known in business circles as low overhead. The unreliable relics on which his livelihood depended required constant tinkering but no bank loan payments. The constant downtime cut into his profits, but then, the need for profit was smaller than usual. You can get by on very little as long as you don't need much and, more importantly, know how to tell the difference between your needs and your wants.

There is also something to be said for being responsible for your own livelihood, hardscrabble as that living may be. What he did every day wasn't really an economic enterprise, but rather, an art form. Any fool with no talent and a hundred million dollars can be efficient. But doing good work on a shoestring budget requires both of Thomas Edison's basic elements of genius—perspiration and inspiration—in spades. For forty years the Old Man did the impossible every day. It was complex, challenging and thoroughly satisfying work. It was also utterly human and humane.

People, it has been demonstrated, just aren't efficient. At best, we can maintain about 60 percent efficiency at work—thirty-six of every sixty minutes per working hour earning our pay. (The other twenty-four minutes we spend maintaining our sanity.) This is why corporations (which are themselves beings as artificial and nonhuman as any robot) are so fond of machinery and so ready to "outplace" workers, replacing them with laser scanners, computers and hydraulic cylinders. Ever increasing productivity looks great on a spreadsheet or tucked into a quarterly report, though it's hell for people, families, communities and the land.

What people do best is the impossible, creatively balancing a wide range of conflicting concerns, desires and obstacles to achieve a complex set of goals. When a machine encounters a paradox it ceases to function; people just shrug, laugh and carry on. Researchers in artificial intelligence (an obvious oxymoron) strive to teach a machine to play a decent game of chess. Personally, I'd be more impressed if they could teach one to handle something truly difficult like surviving puberty or divorce.

It is a rare thing in the timber industry of the 1990s for a man and an employee or two to fall, log, haul, mill and sell a particular stick of wood. It would be foolhardy to compete with the specialized links that form an efficient chain to carry out that process. Rare now too are the celebrated virtues of the gyppo, though fifty years ago they were unremarkable, as unnoticed as, say, old growth forest, clean water and healthy salmon runs.

Time, we say, is money, meaning that spending the least time earning the most money is a standard to measure our success. Ultimately, by this logic, the highest success is to spend no time at all doing useful work and to receive more than we could possibly spend for doing so. Only on the Big Rock Candy Mountain.

To the productivity expert, pursuing the corporate dream (if "an agreed upon legal fiction" can be said to dream) of 100 percent efficient workers, there is never enough time. Squeezing one more marketable unit out of a day only leads to efforts to increase that amount, however fractionally. The hallmark of artists is that they always have plenty of time.

Clason had time, time to fix whatever was broken at the moment, time to sit talking with an old friend who'd dropped by, time to wait for the weather to cooperate, time for a catnap every day after lunch, and, always, plenty of time to do a job right.

Doing a good job cost him plenty over the years but he stubbornly insisted on it. I'd hate to characterize him as an idealist, but he did everything conscientiously and derived a lot of pride from that. He was, I think, wise enough to understand that pride was about all his show ran on. Taking a few extra minutes to ensure that he did as little damage as possible to the land came as naturally to him as ensuring his own safety. Time, he had to spare, and so losing a few hours in the course of a job was cheaper, in the long run, than losing his self-respect.

What, in the end, made a quaint anachronism out of Stewart Clason was that he kept doing the same supremely human thing, practicing an art, while all around him logging and milling steadily shifted away from being a unique art form to just another increasingly efficient industrial process.

"It's a trade-off," he told me one unexpectedly balmy January day. "Sure, I could make big money. Work as a millwright maybe, or a supervisor for some big outfit somewheres. But then, I wouldn't have time to sit here drinking coffee and listening to them frogs singing about spring. You've either got the time or the money, but you never have both."

His time is gone now. I guess that's what made me pause for a moment to consider the history of an old rough-cut cedar board that was now useless except to light a hearth fire in my home.

In his time the Old Man survived the Great Depression, combat in Europe, a half-dozen severe housing slumps, a hard-fought, violent (and futile) timber faller's strike and the daily risk of death or crippling injury. Using his wits, his muscles and his integrity he supported a wife and four children, taught his two sons the trade he'd learned from his father and grandfather and made himself useful to everyone around him in uncountable, often charitable, ways.

He survived long enough to play with his grandchildren and to become an anachronism. He lived to see his years of struggling against corporate perfidy ignored by a society in which the proud title of logger had become a term of disdain, while the very corporations that had made him obsolete used his and his fellow gyppos' lives as an example of what they hoped to preserve by cutting too much timber much too quickly. With old age, he found himself in a world that didn't have a place for him and his kind. And yet, this unkind cut, too, he accepted philosophically, fully aware of the injustice and ornery as ever. He'd never expected much, never wanted much and never had a whole lot to show for his labors. But he kept working anyway.

We talked of death one day, on a landing up on Tater Hill where we were salvaging cull logs left behind on a clearcut. He'd been down in the hole all morning, bucking logs and setting chokers while I ran the jury-rigged old Dodge that served as our yarder and skidder. A half-hour shy of noon, a heavier than usual log hung itself up against a stump, the engine slowed and then stalled. Stewart hand-signaled "slack line" and then "shut down," drawing a knife-finger across his throat, and trudged up to the landing with his chainsaw. "Well, the mule quit on us," he said, "must be dinner time."

We sat in the shade on the edge of the cut, ate our lunch and talked "of shoes and ships and sealing wax and cabbages and kings" as we did every day. I told a story about a clumsy roofer I'd worked with in New Mexico. The Old Man sat stretched out with his back against a tree trunk preparing for a nap. Years of familiarity with sudden violent death, in combat and at work, had reconciled him to the notion that one could be alive one moment and a lifeless mess the next. He confessed, though, a deep fear of dying slowly, lingering on in a living death from cancer as many of his relatives and friends had done.

"When I go," he allowed, "I want it to be just like this, stretched out in the woods somewhere on a nice day with my eyes closed."

In the end, six years later, he died of a heart attack while fishing for trout at Crane Prairie Reservoir, alive and joking one moment and stretched out on the dock with his eyes closed the next.

Robert Leo Heilman

Robert Leo Heilman is a writer from Myrtle Creek, Oregon. His first book, *Overstory Zero; Real Life in Timber Country*, a collection of essays, was published by Sasquatch Books in 1995. Heilman is a Contract Advisor for the Oregon Local of the National Writers Union.

This essay appeared in the Summer 1996 issue of *Oregon Quarterly*.

The Last Log

Ellen Waterston

A simple ritual honors the end of an era.

On September 9, 1993, a Crown Pacific "Memo to Employees" announced that the last large log would be processed through the mill that day at noon, signaling the final closure of that portion of mill operations.

The informal plan was to allow station operators the opportunity to perform their task one last time—loader, trimmer, debarker, scaler, sawyer, edger, filer, green chain puller, stacker and planer. It is not clear whether the mill management realized how important this impromptu ceremony would prove to be. Western corporate culture isn't known for recognizing the need for rituals—to celebrate beginnings, to give thanks, to grieve endings. Likewise, millworkers and loggers aren't credited for placing much stock in such events. And anyway, who would have thought this day would ever come?

After all, since 1915, lumber mills had defined Bend's skyline—towering smokestacks, massive wooden basilicas, wigwam burners and railroad transoms. The timber industry provided the economic blood that gave life to the young town, attracting scores of workers from the Midwest—family man and outdoorsman, adventurer and artisan—to fell trees or process logs. Work in the woods and in the mills was a way of being that boasted its own language, dress and customs, and had put bread on the tables of generations of Central Oregonians.

In 1984 the city of Bend requested that the mill stop sounding the shift whistle because of the number of complaints from white-collar new-comers to the growing community. When the whistle fell dumb, little did anyone realize what that silence forebode. This was still well before the spotted owl was a subject of household debate; before Earth First! radicals were sinking shards of metal into tree trunks to intentionally cause injury, or even death, to the logger when his saw struck the rogue metal; before zealots were camped in treetops, a human sacrifice to the preservation of a tree.

But sure enough, nine years later in August of 1993, Crown Pacific was forced to announce the closure of the large log portion of the Bend mill. It seemed every day that year a mill closed somewhere in Oregon, economically and emotionally crippling entire communities overnight. In Bend, local workers and loggers alike wanted to believe that at least the small mill portion of the Bend operation would continue to run. But anyone who took the time could see that the supply of raw material, re-gardless of the stump diameter, was dwindling because of stricter and stricter enforcement of cutting regulations, and that environmental victo-ries had resulted in the prohibition of logging across enormous tracts of federal forest throughout the region.

The small mill would close four months later.

The day the last large log was milled was almost disrespectful in its sunny, crisp, carefree giddiness, as days in that high desert community are at that time of year. The gigantic, yellow front-end loader, gripping the enormous girth of the Ponderosa in its talons, waddled on its massive cat tracks toward the belt that would receive the log and start it on its journey through the mill. Men in work boots, t-shirts and overalls lined the ramp that skirted the belt, watching in respectful silence. The log crashed mightily down off the loader into the cradle of the conveyor. The gears were thrust into forward, the wheels and cogs reluctantly starting to turn, screeching and wailing in protest—as if they knew.

The log was forced through the trimmer and debarker, emerging white and pure, its round promise coming to a stop at the entrance to the dark interior of the mill. The conveyor belt was abruptly shut down, whining to a halt. Then, in startling silence, uninterrupted, not even by a cough or shuffle of feet, eighty-eight-year-old former forester Hans Milius stepped up to scale the log. In his hand he held a long, wooden measuring device with a sharp hook on one end, designed to grab the outside of the log. As the acknowledged elder designated to reside over the log's last rites, he solemnly and deliberately called out the log's dimensions. He then passed the measuring stick, like a runner in a slow motion relay, to another and then another, each younger than the previous—so that all those who had ever done this job could have their final turn, confirming, as Hans had, that this was a big, beautiful and generous pine, whose bounty would raise many a roof in and around the Northwest.

Just as suddenly the belt was started up again, and this time the head sawyers took turns slicing the log into boards. The first stepped into the glassine-covered booth that looked like the control cab of a ferris wheel. He took pains to carefully hone straight dimensions, swiveling on the chair, deftly wielding the gears, as the log rocked dumbly back and forth, boards separating from the motherlode. And then, as though choreographed in advance, the next sawyer and then another wordlessly stepped in behind, taking a last turn at the task that had for years meant clothes for the kids, a new ski boat, a pickup truck, the dishes the wife wanted, the La-Z-Boy, a VCR, tuition for the first in the family to attend college, or Saturday nights at the show.

Working in a small garret above were the band-saw filers. The thirty-foot-long steel saw below them spun faster than the speed of sight, its offset metallic teeth gnawing furiously and surgically through the center of the log. Replacement blades lay waiting, loose and languid on the floor of the dimly lit work space.

Ellen Waterston

The specialized skill of the band-saw sharpener determined the kerf, or width, of the saw cut. The wider, the more waste. Every filer prided himself on his own technique for producing the thinnest possible kerf. Like everyone who worked the mills, he knew there was no place for waste in this profession. Tuned, the freshly sharpened saw was fed to the sawyer through a hole in the floor of the attic hideaway, then lifted, as limp as a dead man, onto the feeder belt and secured into position. At the flick of the switch the saw leapt back to lethal life, cutting the log cleanly in half again.

At every station the log's significance increased in proportion to its diminishing size. Each time the gears were stopped, the real and symbolic importance of the mighty partnership of man and machine was underscored, framed by a silence as immense as the interior of the mill itself. The working men who crammed the scaffold that crisscrossed the loft of the building wept silently. Stilled, these huge wheels and pulleys were robbed of their empowering companion—like the skeleton of a mastodon robbed of its flesh and breath. The suggestion of power, but only the suggestion, remained. Both the machines and the men were diminished, were less for it. Less machine. Less man.

The log now lay cut into smooth, even, white planks and stacked, ready for the dry kiln. The machines and cranes and saws and belts in the large log mill on the banks of the Deschutes River were silenced forever. But the men assembled there, with no prompting, engaged in a last act of defiance against the course of history. As one, they moved toward the pulley that triggered the shift whistle. They pulled hard on the rope, and the whistle sounded long and sang loud of the machines and the men who operated them, offered shrill thanks to the evergreen forests that surrounded them. When finally it stopped sounding, the men let out a gruff, uneven cheer, tripped up by their emotions, and wordlessly walked out of the building, their tin lunch pails and hard hats in hand.

The next Monday, when they showed up for career counseling, the echo of that whistle rang in their ears, like a promise. It continued to sing in their hearts, as they, in the weeks to come, tried to persuade their strong, thick fingers to dance delicately across a keyboard instead of pulling the green chain. This accidental ritual had allowed them to pay homage to the ending of a way of life that was made of them, powered by them— great men of great action, strength and endurance. They rode the sound of that whistle into the next chapter of their lives not without terrible sadness, but nevertheless comforted in the knowledge that this ending had been duly honored, ritualized and blessed.

Ellen Waterston is a writer who lives in Bend, Oregon. Her poetry, essays and short stories have appeared in numerous anthologies and reviews, including *West Wind Review, Oregon East, Our Turn, Our Time* and *Woven on the Wind.* She is a produced playwright, the recipient of Fishtrap, Atlantic Center for the Arts and Caldera fellowships and the author of two children's books. Her non-fiction book, *Then There Was No Mountain,* will be published in the fall of 2003 by Roberts Rinehart Publishers.

This essay was the third-place winner in the 2000 *Oregon Quarterly* Northwest Perspectives Essay Contest. It is part of an unpublished collection of short stories and essays, *Where the Crooked River Rises.*

Get Off My Cloud

Steve McQuiddy

*Do Oregonians really hate Californians—or just
all outsiders?*

In Colorado they're called Texans. In the Carolinas, Floridians. In New England they call them "Two-One-Twos," the Manhattan area code. They spread out to the country and buy up the land, driving up the prices so the natives have to leave. They clog the roads with their cars and the air with their cell-phone talk. They come to escape the crime and decay of the place they just left, and then complain that there's nothing to do. They're superficial, competitive and think the environment means the lighting and background music in a restaurant. In northern California they call them Southern Californians. In Oregon we just call them Californians.

At least that's what the survey said.

The Oregonian Survey was created in 1996 by Glenn Tsunokai, a doctoral student in sociology at the University of California, Riverside. Tsunokai had heard the stories of what horrors awaited Golden Staters when they went north, but found no hard research to back it up. So he adapted a questionnaire from the widely accepted General Social Survey and sent it out to 600 Oregon households.

Over half of them replied, nearly double the usual response. Roughly a third called themselves Oregon natives, while about 18 percent named California as their last state of residence. But wherever the respondents originally came from, the results still weren't pretty. Sixty-eight percent said Californians would cause a negative change in their communities. Fifty-three percent said the natural environment will deteriorate if more Californians come. Adjectives chosen to describe Californians included superficial, competitive, impersonal and unconcerned about the environment.

The story hit the news wire and the howl began. "They hate us! They really hate us!" cried the *Los Angeles Times*. A wise-cracking writer for the Riverside *Press Enterprise* shot back, "But, like, we have a way bigger Nordstrom and tons of Starbucks and we recycle more bottles and cans than they do, so, like, what's their problem?" Maybe there is some resentment, pondered a columnist for the *Sacramento Bee*, "But honey, they're still glad to take our money."

Back in Eugene, the *Register-Guard* ran an editorial urging caution. "It's entirely possible that many who responded had some fun with this questionnaire and took it as an opportunity to paint an extreme picture rather than volunteer serious feelings."

Oh yeah? snapped a man in the following spate of letters-to-the-editor of the Eugene paper. Oregonians are the greedy ones, he said, selling their houses for as much as they can get. They don't keep their promises, he added, and they're bad drivers, too.

Bad driver, yourself, countered a woman who related being cut off by a car with California plates.

"Move back to California," wrote a Montana emigrant.

Promises, right, observed a real estate broker come from California three years ago. "I'm amazed at the number of times an Oregonian won't follow through on a promise."

You complainers are why they did the survey in the first place, wrote a native Oregonian. "I don't believe Oregonians are rushing to California to take advantage of the real estate market, nor are they buying up banks—"

STOP! Everybody, stop. Stop and think for a minute. *How in the world did it get this way?*

Enjoy your visit

Most people associate anti-California sentiment with former Governor Tom McCall, a 1936 University of Oregon graduate. During his tenure from 1967–1975, McCall was a powerful defender of Oregon's quality of life, and, for better or worse, is probably best known outside the state for his so-called "visit, but don't stay" speech. Well, it wasn't a speech. And to understand the statement, it helps to know the context.

It was January 1971. McCall had just been re-elected to his second term. Oregon was in good shape economically and had made great strides with its land-use and environmental laws. McCall wanted Oregon to be known forever as a state that prized its livability. Growth was necessary, he believed, but not the kind of growth he'd seen in other regions. When a CBS News reporter asked McCall how he would stop people from coming in, the governor replied, "Come visit us again and again. This is the land of excitement. But for heaven's sake, don't come here to live."

Oregon suddenly became known as the place where they wanted you to leave, and its symbol became the highway sign in the Siskiyou Mountains at the California border: WELCOME TO OREGON. WE HOPE YOU ENJOY YOUR VISIT.

Hogwash, McCall said. Oregon needed people and business coming in, he explained, but not at any price. "Industry must come here on our terms, play the game by our environmental rules and be members of the Oregon family," he said. "We lose some this way—and we want to lose that kind of company."

Responsibility is a risky business, and with the current high-tech boom, we are again facing decisions concerning development, conservation or both. For long-time Oregonians—who have known the good days and the bad—this has never been easy, says Ken Metzler, UO emeritus professor of journalism. "We're caught in the middle, between jobs and the environment, and we're working for something that is a compromise between the two."

A native of Boring, a small town outside of Portland, Metzler has traveled the length and breadth of the state. He spoke with many residents while researching his 1986 book, *The Best of Oregon*. "People who come from California have two reactions," he says. "They can't stand it and go back, or they want to change their lifestyle and preserve what they find." This preservationist attitude taken to the extreme is what some call the "Last Settler Syndrome." The newcomers want to close the door behind them, Metzler writes. "It is they who know how bad things are elsewhere."

Just say Orygone

And it might get that bad here if the crooks get in, said the Blitz-Weinhard television ads of the late 1970s ("Where you boys going with all that beer?") and the recent Washington Mutual commercial in which the Rodeo Grandmas intercept a northbound stagecoach representing a nameless bank ("You all bandits, then?" "No ma'am, we're Californians."). DON'T CALIFORNICATE OREGON bumper stickers sounded the warning for a time. But it was a little stack of greeting cards that captured the Oregon spirit in the early 1970s.

Oregon Ungreeting Cards were the inspiration of the late Frank Beeson, a 1959 UO graduate, who brought in James Cloutier (a 1962 graduate who got his MFA in 1969) to do the artwork. Featuring a stout, round-headed fellow with a raincoat and umbrella, the cards ran gags based on Oregonian clichés—rain, anti-tourism, small towns and backward attitudes. They were a smash: Sales topped 20,000, and one cartoon was featured in a 1974 issue of *Newsweek*. "We had more orders than we could keep up with," Cloutier recalls.

They also had no experience in the business. When unsold cards started coming back from California, they learned that the salesman there had sold them on a buy-back guarantee—without telling the Ungreeting folks. "We were buried in returns," Cloutier said in 1976.

Cloutier's spin-off projects fared better. The Society of Native Oregon Born (SNOB) has almost 5,000 members to date, and his *Orygone* cartoon joke books are still asked for in some bookstores. Cloutier tells how he stumbled into a television camera crew while delivering his first *Orygone* press run to Portland in December 1977. A buzz had started with an advance review and so he simply handed a copy to the reporter. "He starts reading the book and he cracks up," Cloutier says. "The camera's going and so that's on the six o'clock news." He sold 15,000 books in the three weeks leading up to Christmas.

But when he later tried the same thing California-style, he may as well have tossed his books into the La Brea tar pits. Maybe what Cloutier termed "negative provincial humor" didn't sit so well down south, or maybe it was because some stores mistakenly put the joke book in the travel section—but the California version did not sell. "Maybe California is enough of a joke in itself," Cloutier says with a smile.

Goths and Vandals

California is where you *want* to go, said popular Oregon writer and historian Stewart Holbrook during the 1950s. Pointing out the sunshine and easy welfare of California, Holbrook—a New England emigrant—tirelessly reminded all who would listen that the Northwest was not where they wanted to be. Rain and the dull-headedness of the natives will bore you to death, he said, and the nuclear reactor at Hanford will eventually make every male in the Northwest sterile. "According to my record book, I alone was responsible that a few more than two hundred homeseeking families did not settle, as they had planned, in Oregon, but chose California instead," he wrote in 1962.

As to his founding of the James G. Blaine Association, whose members devoted themselves to discouraging "the hordes of Goths and Vandals who have been touring our blessed region," Holbrook wrote, "it has no connection whatsoever with the man who was once a senator from Maine. It merely struck me as having the right antique flavor to confuse the public into thinking us a crowd of old-time fuddy-duddies, still living in the past."

"Living in the past" may have been uttered tongue-in-cheek, but the past holds some real weight in Oregon, illustrated by what Holbrook called the Pioneer Cult. Oregonians had no *Mayflower*, but they had the covered wagon, he wrote. "A cult naturally grew from the symbol, and took form in pioneer associations. Membership in these groups was predicated on the time of arrival." Its mild snobbism is harmless, for it has its foundations in one of the greatest American experiences, he said. "It is a heritage infinitely finer than 'blood' or 'gentle birth.'"

Knowing your heritage—or at least your territory—can be useful, says Melody Ward Leslie, a fourth-generation Oregonian and a 1979 UO graduate. Hailing from "Doodle Hollow," a former lumber camp along the Coquille River outside Bandon, Leslie mentions the record-setting rainfall and floods of 1996. "I've seen the luxury homes going up along the rivers, and thought: No old-timer would build a house there." Then she laughs and adds, "But probably an Oregonian sold that land to them."

Development is inevitable, but it doesn't all have to be concrete, Leslie says. She tells of one family returning to Oregon after a generation or two in California. They bought some land in her hometown area and are developing it with respect for the environment. They are not attempting to conquer the river and are paying attention to how their construction will affect their neighbors—before they build. "If that is how Californians are going to behave, then I'm a very happy Oregonian."

Then there are the more urban immigrants, who may have simply moved here for a job. They drive from their condo in Running Water Estates to the new Shopping Depot Super Center, without ever knowing that just last year Canada geese were landing in what is now their planned community's Nautilus and sauna room. "They're contributing to a kind of unwitting obliteration," Leslie says. "They may not mean any harm; they just don't know anything else."

The green and the gold

Which brings us to the fork in the road. There's a place along the Oregon Trail, outside Fort Hall in southeastern Idaho, where the settlers turned north or south. Legend says that the route north was marked by a sign that said TO OREGON, and the road south was identified by a small pile of fool's gold. The ones who could read continued on to Paradise. The greedy and illiterate went to California.

Literate or not, the bulk of Americans who headed for Oregon in the 1840s were looking for land and a place to put down roots. Rich or poor when they arrived, they at least shared a common possibility for the future, and on that note were equals. It bred, rather than class consciousness, a sense that any one person is as good as any other, and gave rise to the notions of individual freedom and tolerance for which Oregon has—paradoxically, perhaps—come to be known.

The early Oregon histories are brimming with the contradictory nature of the territory's settlement. There's John McLoughlin, the "Father of Oregon," who arrived in the early 1800s. Known far and wide for his integrity and compassion, he was actually in the employ of the British-owned Hudson's Bay Company, and ordered to keep American settlers out. Boston schoolteacher Hall Jackson Kelley, whose soaring and sometimes purple prose was credited with initiating the original "Oregon Fever," only visited the region once. And what people saw in the land was, often as not, conflicting. "Perhaps there is no country in the world that offers more inducements to enterprise and industry than Oregon," wrote one town-builder. But another writer said of an old Oregon pioneer, "He is living in the valley of the Willamette, where, doubtless, he is now chafing under the affliction of having neighbors in the same region, and nothing but an ocean beyond."

There's a kind of schizophrenia about the state, an attempt to reconcile the impulse to tell others of Paradise with the sometimes urgent need to protect it from them. And yet, the 1974 *Newsweek* article, titled "Where the Future Works," observed of Oregonians, "What motivates them is no antipathy to private enterprise, progress or growth, but something subtler—a long-building and overriding sense of collective responsibility that doesn't seem to exist in many other places."

World enough and time

And here we are. Oregon is again one of the hottest spots in the country. Again, it is time to change. Portland and its environs are already being called "The Silicon Forest." Interstate 5 through Salem is eerily reminiscent of the strands of freeway lacing San Jose. Eugene looks like it's been taking Palo Alto lessons. Bend is turning into a Disneyland of resort castles surrounded by trailer parks and cubicles housing the people who serve the guests. What kind of change will it be?

"I see it happening and I wonder what it must have been like for the native people when they saw us coming with our ships and wagons and guns," says Melody Ward Leslie. "And I feel a kinship with them—which is ironic, because my people used to have the Indians do their laundry and garden chores."

Development scares the hell out of Oregonians, says Ken Metzler. "As long as we don't vote down the land-use laws, I think we're in pretty good shape." He pauses a moment. "But if it doesn't hold, then I'm bothered."

It is not a state that Oregonians appear to dread, so much as it is a state of mind. For every one of us here now, someone or something came before—and perhaps that fact is lost in our hurry to make our own lives more comfortable. Driving the roads of Oregon today, it is easy to forget that it all began more than 10,000 years ago, writes Terence O'Donnell in the history section of the 1997 *Oregon Blue Book*. "Cruising the freeway hardly brings to mind those first 100 centuries of native life, only in detail different from our own, at bottom the same—shelter, food, some ornament and myth, birth, growing and decay."

The changes since that time have been rapid, and ever more rapid, more and more each year, O'Donnell reminds us. "And before we know it we are flying down the freeway, gazing out across this time-deep land where, as we sometimes forget, so much has happened."

Steve McQuiddy is a Eugene-based writer who moved to Oregon in 1981 from the East Coast. He has visited California many times.

This essay appeared in the Spring 1997 issue of *Oregon Quarterly*.

Migration

Leslie Leyland Fields

The journey from here to there teaches us where we are,
but the lessons always cost.

Every August, the short-tailed shearwaters come—swarms, thousands uncountable into Uyak Bay and along the west side of Kodiak Island and the Aleutians. They are not majestic; they are small and sooty black and move in not with a brooding presence, but a shrill gaiety. I thought little of them for a number of years, until I discovered their genius and endurance. When they arrive, chattering and giddy as though returning from a cocktail party, they are in fact celebrating perhaps the first rest stop in a 6,000-mile race that will take them from northern Alaska to Australia one wingbeat at a time.

And the salmon, of course, swarms as uncountable, are making migratory journeys of their own that still stun us in their duration and accuracy: A salmon often will return from years in the open ocean to locate the very stream of its birth.

I migrate to this place too, in a flock of my own making, with my husband, Duncan, and six children, ages one to fourteen. In the scheme of migrations, our trip is trivial—a mere 100 miles. We move between islands, between our winter home on Kodiak Island in the Gulf of Alaska and our summer camp on a tiny, remote island off the larger island's west side, where we fish commercially for salmon. How small the distance, the length of an eyelash on a state map. On a national map, a distance that doesn't exist. How simple—and yet, not. Like the salmon and the shear-waters, we must take to the air and water to get there. For all of us, the distance brings dangers. But however perilous the migration for the salmon and the shearwaters, they make it look so simple, so graceful, their arrival to this country so inevitable. None of this is true for us.

It is September. We have been married three years. Everyone is gone but three of us—Duncan, my father-in-law DeWitt, and myself. We are the stay-behinds, the ones to close up camp. When we are done, we will make our migratory return to Kodiak, this year in the speedboat, a twenty-five-foot Mako, a v-bottomed hull with twin 140s that take our breath away when opened up on flat water. The others had gone by plane, the usual mode, but the Mako had to return to town for the winter, and logically, the last ones to go would take it. With a top speed of forty miles per hour, we could theoretically make it to town in just under three hours— as opposed to twelve hours or longer on a larger fishing boat.

The route from our island to the town of Kodiak is semi-circular, beginning on the west side of mostly roadless Kodiak Island, heading northeast through the Shelikof Strait, past deep fjord-like bays named Uganik, Viekoda, Kizhuyak, Monashka—then squeezing through Whale Pass, a Scylla and Charybdis passage where the tide muscles through in bulges and whirlpools, then out to the open waters of the Gulf of Alaska and the final curve south into Kodiak.

At six in the morning, the weather report on the marine radio was not favorable, but the water was calm as we looked out toward the Shelikof Strait. We could see some twenty miles and the going looked good, and after a long summer at fish camp the rest of our lives awaited us. We would go. All we needed was three hours to sneak around the corner into town.

It was a gray day, as so many are, the water and sky and clouds all different textures of the same color. The run out into the Shelikof for the first ten miles was good. We were prepared for the trip, dressed warmly in layers of thermals and sweatshirts, each with a long-billed baseball hat to shield our eyes from wind and spray and hood tied tightly to secure it; then wool socks, rubber hip boots and, last, heavy rain gear to break the wind and keep us dry. Duncan was driving; DeWitt and I stood, holding on to the frame of the console. With 280-horsepower, we could move, but seldom smoothly. And there were no seats. We had taken out the one seat in front of the wheel, a leftover artifact from Florida, where the boat had come from. The idea of lounging on a cushioned seat while driving was as unthinkable to us as throwing out a line and water skiing in shorts. We held tight but kept our legs loose to absorb the shock of every impact and huddled our heads behind the windshield.

Not long after we rounded Cape Kuliak, the weather made good on the forecast. No rain, but the wind began almost as though a starting gun had been fired: from breathless to a stiff twenty-knot breeze almost instantly; from level waters to whitecaps in a moment. And once started, momentum balled it all to twelve-foot waves, a thirty-five-knot north-easterly wind, and we were bucking into it, already thinking about turning back.

We began to confer on this idea, which was not as simple as it appeared: We were about halfway between places of shelter. Before a decision, the rumbling engines suddenly gargled—and then, a loud thwack. We turned, already suspecting the culprit. These engines had broken down before. Yet one of our crew, a fair mechanic, had worked them over thoroughly and guaranteed their trip-worthiness. We scuttled to new stations. DeWitt took the helm while Duncan gave a quick inspection and I stood ready with the toolbox. The diagnosis was quick and painful—a rod had

Leslie Leyland Fields

been thrown. We still had the other 140-horse, and then a kicker, 35-horsepower, as another backup. But the one engine couldn't lift us onto the steppe, the level at which the boat cruises efficiently. We were heavy in the water, with the three of us and our gear, and could eke out just enough speed to keep the bow into the waves, but we rode the worst of every one.

It was clear by now that we needed to turn around and head back to the island. We had no sooner begun to turn, cautiously, so as not to be caught in the roll of the waves, when the bilge pump gave out. The water that was washing over us and pouring into the bilge now had nowhere to go. Within a few minutes, our limp became a crawl.

"Put your survival suits on!" Duncan yelled above the wind. It was an acknowledgment of emergency that suddenly sped everything to a fast-forward blur: our awkward clamber into our oversized neoprene suits; the boat nearly dead in the water, rolling in every surge, threatening to turn sideways in the twelve-foot waves; sheets of ocean pummeling us; Duncan bent over the pump; DeWitt trying to control the boat; me clinging to the console to keep from washing overboard. But even then I had hope. Something in me trusted—until Duncan leaned over and shouted in a shrill voice to be heard through the hooded suit: "Leslie, if we don't get out of this, I want you to know how much I love you!"

I think this was meant as reassurance. And despite our steady and rapid progression to this state of affairs, I was not yet truly afraid. But Duncan's message was the final stamp of emergency with only two outcomes possible: that we would survive or we would not. I realized the full extent of our situation. No one knew where we were. We had no radio or means of contacting anyone. We were more than a mile from shore, and the shoreline was nothing but vertical cliffs. Rescuing planes could not fly. I began to pray.

Duncan and DeWitt kept frantically working, tinkering, and some minutes later, water began sputtering out of the bilge hose again. The pump was functioning, but no one whooped or celebrated. There were still too many ifs. The Mako, near lifeless, did not respond immediately to the now functioning pump. It was a slow pump and far too much water had filled the hull. Yet slowly, gradually, the boat began to respond to the rudder and nose back into the oncoming waves, wounded, unsteady, but capable now of direction.

The three of us returned to the console, holding on as before, but tighter, and all of us leaning forward, urging ourselves through the Shelikof Strait. We headed for Uganik Bay, just the next bay over from Uyak. On a calm day in a healthy speedboat, the trip there would have taken just forty minutes. Today, it was three hours. We slogged our way in to Village Island, where a friend lived, an Eskimo homesteader named Daniel Boone Reed. We were exhausted, quiet as we peeled off our survival suits. Only our eyes and noses had been exposed, the suits sealing off any entrance of water, yet through that minuscule space came enough water to saturate our layers of clothing, to drench us to the skin.

Our options for coming and going to our fish camp were wisely cut by one.

That did not end, of course, the dilemma of ways and means of our migrations from the town of Kodiak out to our island. We may make the trip three times a year or only once or maybe four times, but each one takes us into a vale of decisions and calculations.

One year, still before children, we faced the same question with a different set of variables. Duncan and I had spent the winter there on the island, just the two of us. For that year and a half, we had moved our valuables and necessities out with us, all the verifications of our personhood: birth certificates, marriage license, passports, photos of our recent travels through Africa, boxes of tax documentation and three boxes of my writings. When it was time to return to town, we decided that flying was too risky for our belongings. It all sounds so illogical now, but in the previous eight years, there had been four fatal small plane crashes, all pilots we knew and had flown with. It took no imagination to visualize the cargo of our vital statistics in an ugly conflagration amid a smoldering wreck.

Thankfully and somewhat inexplicably, these visions never included me. So I would fly since I was on my way out to visit my family back east. Duncan and our valuables would go by boat, with a friend who had offered a free trip to Kodiak on his crab boat, the *Mary M.*

The drama began, as Duncan told me later, close to midnight. They were several hours into the trip, about halfway down the Shelikof Strait. There were three of them, the couple who owned and fished the boat and Duncan, and then about fifteen dogs, representing only half of this couple's surrogate children. The rest were back at the cannery where they had been winter watchmen for ten years. The seas weren't particularly rough, but during one person's wheel watch, the boat began handling strangely, sluggishly, taking too long to rise from the trough of the waves. A quick run out to the deck confirmed the worst: The stern was so low in the water the deck was awash. The other two were sleeping and awoke to shouts and barking. It was too late for anything but a mayday, survival suits and the life raft.

Back in New Hampshire, it was 4 A.M. I was in the extra bedroom in my mother's house. I was worn out from the trip there, thirty-six hours of airplanes and airports, but still, it was hard to sleep. My life was about to change forever. And no one knew yet. We had waited eight years to begin a family. Finally we both felt ready for children, but, predictably, nothing happened. Nothing happened for nearly two years. We were in the first stages of infertility testing and were discussing adoption when the white strip finally turned blue. I found out that first night at my mother's that we were indeed pregnant.

Later that morning, at about ten, the phone rang. It was Duncan. My mother handed me the phone, and I swallowed hard, wondering whether or not to tell him now, over the phone.

"Hello!" I greeted in a cheery voice. Silence. Then, "Leslie?" in a small voice that didn't sound like Duncan's. "Yes?" I answered, alarmed. Something was wrong. "What is it, Duncan?"

"The boat sank," he said in a shaky voice.

Migration   **80**

"What? Are you all right? Where are you calling from?"

"I'm all right. I'm here at my parent's, house. We lost everything on the boat, though." And then he stopped, and suddenly I heard him sobbing great deep sobs.

I sat down, stunned with the news. In those next few moments, as the night's events spilled out, I watched the sinking, the three of them abandoning ship, the final grotesque roll of the hull and the whirl of the waters that sealed over the dogs and all our belongings, yet irrationally fearing that if I recreated it too vividly, it could turn out differently. They didn't get their survival suits on, the life raft wouldn't inflate, they couldn't free themselves from the rigging when the boat went down, no one heard the mayday, no one picked them up in the life raft. . . . I am widowed at age thirty. The night I find out I am pregnant my husband drowns in a shipwreck. He would never have known about the baby.

We were on the phone a long time. Duncan wouldn't stop apologizing for losing everything—the greatest loss of all, he knew, was the journals and all my writings since childhood. But at that moment, it was I who flung it all in the ocean. It was my conscious, willing choice. In the logic of those moments, it was simple—either my husband or my things.

I didn't tell him that morning that we were pregnant. It was enough to feel the sting of almost-death, to cry together, to thank God. And as I stood among my family in New Hampshire that day, so close to near-loss, I felt so keenly how utterly different my life had become from theirs.

The choices now are mostly two, both variations on a bush plane. We either charter a Widgeon—an amphibious plane from World War II that sports both floats and wheels—out to the island and land right there on our own beach, a luxury that costs $700. Or, the more common practice, is to take the mail plane, a ten-seater Caravan, to the village of Larsen Bay, with a gravel strip, then wait at the cannery for a skiff and a thirty-minute ride out to the island.

Leslie Leyland Fields

It's not a particularly complex itinerary, as bush travel goes, but even on the best of days, I can never shake the weight of the logistics and the whim and the power of the forces around us. Duncan always goes out to the island two weeks ahead of time, so I usually travel alone with the kids. We hope to make it the first try, but the day we are scheduled to leave town may be the fourth day of drenching rains and low clouds. Across the mountains, eighty air miles away, the sun may be shining on our island, but we can't get there. When it finally clears in town and we make one final dash to the airport—the plane is going whether we're on it or not— we discover that the weather has closed in over the mountain passes between here and there. The last plane couldn't make it through and had to come back. Or, we tumble into the trailer-like terminal, all seven of us with bags and backpacks hanging from every hand, ready to squeeze into the plane when we hear the west side has just been hit by a stiff southwest wind, blowing forty and the forecast is for sixty. We go home again. Or, we take off anyway, hoping to beat it, and we hit fog. The ceiling lowers with every mile, until we come to the crucial passes and the pilot can't get through, so he heads out for the water, and our thirty-five-minute crow's flight becomes a fifty-five-minute gull's dip-and-bob along a barely visible shoreline.

No matter how tired I am, I am awake through it all, no matter what the conditions, my energy part of the fuel that powers the plane and propels the skiff. The mountains are always just feet beneath us, the glaciers and lakes touchable. My children surround me with their excitement and questions while the wind buffets us yet closer to the mountainside, nearly grazing the rocks. We make it, land on the gravel strip and hope someone will give us and our forty boxes of baggage a ride down to the cannery where we will wait for Duncan to come in the skiff. He comes. We load the boxes, then many times over I am suiting in rain gear and life jackets, zipping each one snug to the chin and cinching the waists, seating each one in the appropriate spot for the weather. The baby will sit on my lap, the two-year-old cinched next to me with my arm ready to support him when he falls asleep, the next two, seven and nine, both sitting on the outside, hanging out over the water, despite my continued warnings. The older two, thirteen and fourteen, stand in the bow, faces open to the spray and wind.

And sometimes all the variables converge and the sky is bright and the going is swift and the view from the plane is as startling as the day I first came, so that later, heading to the island in the skiff, I want to cry because of this unexpected life I have been given—yet for all of this, still there is little pleasure in the trip.

It is a journey, these 100 miles. Travel for all of us in the bush is still a journey, requiring intent, strategy, reservoirs of energy, and faith. And yet it is a journey that locates us, that truly teaches the where of a place. The shearwaters and the salmon above all others know this island. And after twenty-five years of my own migrations, at every arrival, I too know exactly where my island lies.

I say all this in my most philosophical and lyrical moments, when the trip has been good. But in other moments, I would confess my inauthenticity. I am not a real bushwoman, I think, because I do not savor the journey here. It seems noble, somehow, to claim that because we are integrated into the process of traveling, as our ancestors were, that our travels are purer; that rather than being passive we are alive to the miles we pass—we feel them in our stomachs, our heads, the balls of our feet as we balance in the skiff. But we get wet and cold and scared. The miles of wind leave their marks on our faces. The children sometimes cry. People die. This is the truth about our migration.

I would drive a car all the way here if I could. I would take a 747 and sponge back into the seat, flick on the reading light and dive into the novel I'd been waiting to read, oblivious to flight, to arrive at my destination in spite of myself. I do want to be here; I don't always want the getting here. Maybe the short-tailed shearwaters and the salmon feel that way, too.

Leslie Leyland Fields lives in Kodiak, Alaska, where she writes, teaches and runs The Northern Pen, a professional editing business. She is the author of *Surviving the Island of Grace: A Memoir of Alaska* (St. Martins, 2002), *Out on the Deep Blue* (St. Martins, 2001) and *The Entangling Net; Alaska's Commercial Fishing Women Tell Their Lives* (University of Illinois Press, 1996). She can be contacted at <u>northernpen@alaska.com</u>.

This essay is from *Surviving the Island of Grace*. It first appeared in *Oregon Quarterly's* Winter 1997 issue.

Get Off My Log

Kellee Weinhold

Home may be where the heart is, but do we belong?

With September drawing to a close, I have sneaked east, leaving the dampness of the Willamette Valley far behind. Here in Central Oregon only a few clouds have bothered to break up the brilliant blue, the hot air offering little clue that fall has already begun to settle in on the other side of the mountains. The Ponderosa that push close to the road leading to Camp Sherman and the Metolius River filter the still insistent sun, but the smell of several inches of rotting pine needles so common in the spring has been baked into the threatening odor of ready-to-ignite brush.

Amid the heat and dryness of the high-desert side of the Cascades, the Metolius is the essence of cool repose. The headwaters gush to the surface at a consistent forty-eight degrees from an underground spring near the base of Black Butte. Conifers crowd against sedge, alder and willow, which in turn shelter grasses at the river's edge, filtering the heat and pulsing with the steady heartbeat of the water. As riffles of light blue tumble into pools of near green, the river meanders through its basin before growing larger, faster and colder as tributaries join it on the way to Lake Billy

Chinook. Other rivers over here are spring-fed, but the Metolius is the largest and its waters by far the clearest. In the morning, when mist hangs just above the surface and the wild lupine are covered with dew, it is easy to believe that magic lives here.

Easing past familiar landmarks—a smattering of houses, llamas, the fire station, the community center—I scan the landscape. I am looking for damage. Not from forest fire or flood, but damage I am sure has been wrought by a *Sunset* magazine article, now three months old, beckoning its readers to "The Mellow Metolius," the river I have called home for more than a quarter of a century.

I was not born here. I have never lived here. In fact, seven days is the longest I have ever stayed. But when I make that turn off Highway 20, I am returning to the place I am convinced my cells came from.

Perhaps my mother visited here during her pregnancy. Did she drink from the clear water, absorbing its hydrogen and oxygen, her body ultimately reworking the molecules as part of me? Did my father in his years of traipsing the woods of Oregon one day work this red clay dust into his pores, so completely absorbing the essence of the place that it is now part of my genetic makeup?

There is no direct line to trace my belonging, but this valley—where Camp Sherman nestles amid Black Butte, the Green Ridge fault scarp, the Cascade skyline and the forested foothills—is as much a part of me as the Rogue Valley, where I grew up. I have traveled this road countless times seeking the solitude the Metolius offers.

Within minutes, the river is near, and for the first time, my anticipation is weighted with dread. Are there any new houses? Are the signs larger or fancier, redesigned to direct the hordes of tourists embraced by *Sunset*'s welcome? For a brief moment, I consider those people like me who have seen their sacred places touted in "The Magazine for Western Living," but quickly push them aside. This is not the time to wonder why I am irritated with a magazine that any other time I am delighted to receive and whose getaways I have enjoyed.

Instead, I persuade myself that the sign for Cold Water Springs Resort, an RV and tent campground, has gotten bigger and the narrow bridge across the river to the Camp Sherman Store more crowded. The combination general store and fly-fishing outpost, solidly planted at the intersection of various forest roads, fits easily amid the decades-old summer fishing cabins that dot both sides of the river. If there were a center of town, this would be it. It is comforting in its sameness.

The parking lot is full, and I look quickly for California plates, though truth be told they are far from the majority. Travelers from as far away as Arizona and as close as Bend offer testament to the lure of this place. A place where the Tenino and Northern Paiute hunted, fished and gathered food, and 19th century Sherman County farmers traveled by wagon to seek respite in the meadows and forests along the river's banks. I imagine myself to be like them—holding claim to the river simply by having slept alongside it.

But in reality, I rarely camp on the Metolius anymore. The vehicle-friendly campgrounds are too crowded, and as much I would like to pretend otherwise, these days I am a car camper. I like drinkable water and bathrooms close at hand. While some of the backcountry campgrounds offer both, they're a fair walk from the campsites, and unlit. It's dark out there at night. Very dark. But the stars are incredible.

These days, I stay in one of the luxury cabins across the river from the store. Fully equipped, they were designed to blend into the landscape, yet they exude none of the rustic charm of the summer cabins. Rather, they promise all of the comforts of home with the river visible from the deck. So, I sit by the river, walk by the river, scoop water to keep at home as a reminder of this place, but I no longer sleep by the river. Each time I visit and I see more people, I resolve to return to the more isolated backpacking adventures of my youth.

I watch people come and go across the front porch of the store where locals stop briefly to catch up on news, and visitors hand out sodas to small children grubby with outdoor adventure. The familiar thud of hiking boots on the wooden floorboards and the jingle of the bell both draw and repel me. As much as I long to go inside and wander the aisles, studying the collection of photos of those able to capture one of the river's notoriously crafty fish, I resist being counted among these milling tourists.

This time, the number of suntanned *Sunset* types crowding the parking lot on this fall Saturday seems more like a July weekend, when tourists staying in nearby Sisters and Bend come to escape. Although I know the increasing congestion here has little to do with a single article in a magazine and more to do with the sheer numbers of people who like to experience nature, I am determined to lay blame. I cling to the idea that some places should remain untrampled, all the while ignoring the question of why I should be the one to say who can or can't visit.

Since non-native people first saw this river in the 1800s, the "right" to access its magic has been fiercely protected. And I am just one more person who wants to close the door behind me, all the while claiming kinship with those who would have shut it before me had they only had the chance. I resist what I know to be true: These recent "discoverers" feel as much like intruders to me as I do to the people who grabbed up the rights to build summer cabins along this pristine river in the 1900s, and as they do to people of the Confederated Tribes of Warm Springs Reservation who now share rights to approximately 12 miles of this 28-mile river. Each of us wants the Metolius to be the way we remember it.

Wearing my determination in the set of my jaw, I head inside. Roger, who owns the store with his wife, is behind the counter. The people who live here call each other easily by name, their smiles open and inviting. Although I stop short of addressing him, I smile warmly, determined to look as if I belong. My smile brings no more recognition from him than the bland nod of the L.L. Bean-clone who entered in front of me did.

Suddenly embarrassed, I hurry down an aisle toward the display of clothing that sports various incarnations of fish with "Metolius River" or "Camp Sherman" splashed across them. Here among the polar fleece and designer baseball caps, I can hide from the fact that I am indistinguishable from those who have just discovered this "blessed escape." Briefly, I imagine starting a conversation with Roger, letting him know that the first time I remember coming here was in 1972. Back then, most people came to fish. Some people came to camp. I was here with my family the first time, the Youth Conservation Corps the next. We bought handfuls of fish food from a dispenser by the bridge and tossed it into the water. We bought chips and sodas, not the lattes and cream cheese brownies available now. We were not tourists.

Instead, I slip quietly out the door, forgoing the iced coffee I had come in for. Outside, four women—they *must* be Californians—stumble aboard rented mountain bikes. They are varying shades of blonde, evenly tanned and dressed more for a round of golf at Black Butte Resort than a bike trek along dusty roads. Laughing and effervescent, they are the picture of a perfect *Sunset* experience. I scowl and head for the river.

A hike downstream would offer summer cabins on one side and campground after campground on the other, the first few bulging with RVs, then more and more tents the farther from civilization. I head upstream. Though there are summer cabins, they are few. In no time the women and their clamor fade into the background, and I am once again lost in the magic.

The path, used mostly by those who fish the river, hugs its bank, leaving the illusion that the world ends and begins at its shore. For a while nothing intrudes. But in too short a time, I reach the fence that goes not only to the bank but across the river itself. Although the water is the property of the state, the owners can block use of the stream. My brother the hydrologist explains that it has to do with whether the water is "navigable." It looks navigable to me, but I don't make the rules. I want to climb the fence, and continue along the river to its headwaters just a few miles up, but I do not want to be the one caught breaking the rules here. Tourists break rules.

I head to a less-developed road and wander into the woods, listening carefully. The previous year, my partner and I had walked in this same place the week before our wedding. Trudging in the silence that often

Kellee Weinhold

overtakes us here, we heard a whoosh just overhead. Just fifteen feet above us a pair of bald eagles soared along the same road. We stopped, our necks craned to watch them, and then scrambled to keep them in sight as they headed for the river. They felt like a sign, a wedding gift from a loved one. Each time I return, I expect them.

But the eagles do not appear today, and I turn back toward the river's edge. The four women on their rented bicycles are heading toward me on the road. I ignore them and head for the path, where signs forbid bikes The vegetation is fragile, the trail too narrow. They will follow the road, and I will follow the path. I pretend to be absorbed with the river and wait for them to move past in the opposite direction. They have a different plan.

I watch in amazement as the women turn off the road and maneuver their bikes down the path ahead of me, heading back toward the store. They are tentative riders and weave to keep their balance. As I reach the sign they have ridden past, I stop and stare at it, hoping that my intense scrutiny will remind them that they are breaking the rules.

Blissfully unaware of me, they stumble to a stop, drop their bikes onto the ground and climb onto a fallen tree that protrudes into the river. They search for a place to set their camera to capture the moment. I hang back, afraid I will be asked to take the picture. Desperate to berate them for their behavior, I am trapped by social graces and confusion about my place. I simply stare.

I have a picture of myself on that log. A friend took it years ago when we camped downriver, before the luxury cabins were built, before every-thing got so crowded. I visit it every time I come here. I have photos in my office of the river flowing around it, of snow piled on top of it.

These women drive on the shoulder of the road to get ahead of traffic. They have cut me off. They are uninvited guests with their feet propped up on my furniture. They are not this place.

I want them off my log.

Kellee Weinhold is an instructor at the School of Journalism and Communication at the University of Oregon. Her work has appeared in the *Advocate*, the *Oregonian* and gay and lesbian publications across the country.

This essay was a finalist in the 2002 *Oregon Quarterly* Northwest Perspectives Essay Contest.

Another Oregon Trail

Corrina Wycoff

A single mother redefines her American Dream.

I applied for food stamps a few months after my five-year-old son and I moved from Chicago, Illinois, to Eugene, Oregon. On line at the West Eugene Adult and Family Services office, I could barely stand up straight for the weight of my shame. My mother and I had received food stamps when I was a child. They were bulky and large and garish, as if especially designed to attract attention. I had never forgotten how humiliating it felt to stand on the grocery store line, food stamp booklet in hand, between shoppers who paid in cash. I had long ago decided that I would never require food stamps as an adult. I imagined it would be easy to avoid such trappings of poverty. I believed that I would always have a full-time job and that I would never be a single mother.

The West Eugene welfare office sits in a dilapidated shopping center called "The Big Y." Next door to the office stands a check-cashing outpost where one can cash government checks for exorbitant fees, buy money orders and phone cards, and spend an extra fifteen dollars to pay a delinquent bill via Western Union. In the back of the shopping center, behind the hardware store and the Women, Infants and Children (WIC) supply store, one of Oregon's government-run liquor stores does booming business. When I first saw the check cash and the liquor store, I thought, "This is how little faith the culture has in the poor. They think we're suckers and drunks." A notice hanging on the welfare office front door read, "Do not leave your children in your car. It is illegal and carries a $250 fine." Apparently the culture believes that the poor are bad parents, too, and that the only way we won't neglect our children is if we're threatened with fines we can't afford.

Inside the office, people waited on two long lines to check in. I looked at the tattered folding chairs, the mottled linoleum, the dirty toys strewn in corners, and I was glad my son was at kindergarten. I didn't want him to know that I'd come here, that we needed for me to come here. I gave my social security number to the man behind the counter. He typed it into the computer and smiled at me when he said, "You never applied before?"

"No." I shook my head. His smile made me tingle with a fragile, shame-filled pride. I knew it was a gesture of respect I never would have seen if I hadn't come here, and one that I would never see again because I had.

I had almost applied for aid in Chicago. When I was twenty, I lived in a middle-class Chicago neighborhood. I met a middle-class man from a two-parent family and we married, and although I couldn't afford a college education, I got a full-time middle-management job at a school that trained psychoanalysts. I held on to the job and the neighborhood, but my relationship with my husband deteriorated quickly, and I was single by the time my son, Asher, was born in 1994. At that same time, the organization I worked for faced a fiscal crisis and implemented an "austerity budget" that called for increased hours and frozen salaries. I worked ten- and twelve-hour days, carted my son and his cumbersome accoutrements to day care and home on the slow, cold subway because we couldn't afford a car, and spent my nights sitting on the couch, trying to nap in between Asher's frequent feedings and diaper changes.

I was as low on money as I was on energy. After I paid our rent, utilities and childcare each month, I only had $100 left for groceries and other expenses. We never received any child support. I stretched my dollars as far as I could and often felt hungry. It was cost-effective to breastfeed my son, but my own diet didn't provide me with enough nutrition to generate the amount of milk he needed. Eventually, I grew dizzy and my teeth ached each time I fed him or used my breast pump, so, when he was six months old, I began feeding him with formula. This added expense proved too much to bear. Once, a few days before payday, I found myself down to $10. We were almost out of food and formula, completely out of diapers, and my subway fare to and from work and day care was $3.60 a day. Before work the next day, after I dropped off my son at day care, I went to the welfare office.

The Chicago office I visited, situated above a discount furniture store, was hot and noisy and lit with unforgiving yellow light. Plastic chairs stood in cramped rows and every chair was occupied. Some parents held two or three children on their laps. I gave the clerk my name and waited at the edge of the room, near windows that overlooked the street. People stood in a circle on the sidewalk below, trying to warm their bare hands with their breath. Two hours passed and the room grew more crowded. It seemed as if no names were ever called. "How long have you been here?" I asked a woman who fed spoonfuls of mashed banana to a child seated on her lap.

"This is my third day," she answered.

I left the office without seeing a caseworker, went to work, borrowed $20 from my supervisor, and spent it on a canister of formula, a package of diapers, a box of pasta, and a bag of frozen vegetables. Even though the money was borrowed and the food left me hungry, I felt proud to have left that office without officially declaring myself one of the needy. I believed that meant I had a work ethic, that I was a good citizen. It didn't occur to me, then, to ask myself whether my illusory good citizenship prevented me from being a good mother.

Corrina Wycoff

For years, my schedule and our financial problems kept me estranged from my son. Five days a week, he attended day care from seven in the morning until seven or eight at night. I frequently had to work weekends and left him with baby-sitters. It seemed that the kinds of jobs I was qualified for would never provide me with enough money, so I started attending Chicago's public university. I worked full time, attended classes full time, stayed up nights doing homework. I remained a good employee and became a model student. I had a 4.0 grade-point average and managed to complete four years of college in three. Meanwhile, Asher's infancy passed, and I didn't notice any of its milestones. I remember my college essay topics and test scores; I remember how much money I made at work and the projects I chaired. I don't remember Asher's first word or his first step. I don't remember when he began to talk in full sentences or any of the charming toddler things he must have said.

In Oregon, food stamps come in the shape of a debit card. The words, "Oregon Trail" are printed in bold white letters on the front of the card, above the rendering of a covered wagon. It is a paradox that the triumphant mythos of the Oregon Trail on this plastic currency signifies anything but triumph. Perhaps they designed the card as an exhortation; perhaps its implicit message is, "Work hard, be long-suffering, and you too may work toward a life of potential prosperity, selective freedom and colonizing power." Or perhaps the card was designed to shame, to say, "Others pulled themselves up by the bootstraps so why can't you?" Either way, the card seems to suggest that the pioneers of the Oregon Trail and the American Dream they pursued are still viable models for us to follow.

Like many people, my relationship to the American Dream is an ambiguous one. The idea of prosperity at once seduces and repels me. I want prosperity to claim me and sweep me away every bit as much as I want to see it deconstructed, dismantled and exposed.

My behavior indicates that I do subscribe, however critically, to aspects of the American Dream. My son and I moved from Chicago to Eugene in the fall of 1999. I remember how I justified the cross-country move to friends: I would attend graduate school there, my son would begin kindergarten. The public grammar schools would be safer and better than those in Chicago; the cost of living would be cheaper; and my academic success would carry more prestige at my new, more reputable university. What I wanted, then, was no different from the ostensible reasons that drove people west along the Oregon Trail 150 years before. I wanted a better life—a freer, more prosperous, happier life—and I believed I would find one in Oregon. What I found, however, was a different kind of prosperity, one I had never even thought to want. In Oregon, I learned how to be a better mother.

Our apartment was part of the University's family housing system: several blocks of clapboard duplexes and two-story buildings with wide, squat, high windows that trumpeted forgotten decades. In the rental office, the manager handed me my apartment keys and a pamphlet outlining the hazards of lead-based paint. I signed a waiver acknowledging that I'd been told that my walls were poison-coated and that I opted to live between them at my own risk.

"Are people nice here?" I asked. "I mean, is it hard to make friends?"

"Is it hard to make friends in family housing?" The manager laughed. "You don't even have to try."

Carrying sleeping Asher, I walked through the family housing complex to our apartment, but I didn't see any other mothers or kids. Asher woke when we got to our building and started whimpering when I pushed open the apartment door. I wanted to cry too. The ugly outside, painted baby-blue with turquoise trim, was outdone by the cheap, unevenly glossy white paint on the interior walls: a coating as thick and bumpy as an oyster shell. Linoleum tiles, in shades of brown different enough to clash with one another, covered all the floors except the bathroom (in the bathroom were dingy, peach ceramic tiles the color of an aging prom dress), and the rooms were tiny. In addition to beds with sagging, musty, plastic mattresses, the University provided two stained, blue-green plastic chairs, a folding table with rusty metal legs and a narrow couch covered in scratchy brown burlap. The apartment smelled of stagnant dust, and spiders climbed the walls. I told myself it would look better when we unpacked, but I didn't tell Asher that, even though his alarmed eyes told me he could use some comfort. Instead, I tried to sound sincere when I said, "Well, this place is really cute." If I admitted otherwise, I'd also have had to admit that moving was perhaps a huge mistake.

Asher wanted to go outside, to walk around the housing complex and find the nearest playground. Instead, I obsessively went about setting up house. I quickly emptied the boxes I'd shipped. I rented a car, dragged Asher to every resale outpost I could find, and bought rugs, lamps, and bookshelves. The heat and his boredom seemed unimportant. Getting set up, and quickly, eclipsed everything. "Two more stores," I told him, but after those two stores I remembered another errand, then another, then another.

"I hate this," he complained.

I ignored him. "Well, we don't have any food. We have to get some groceries so we can eat tonight."

He looked out the car window. "I'm not hungry."

At the grocery store, I used the very last of my money. I wondered if we would have enough milk and juice to last for two weeks, until I started a full-time job and school and Asher started kindergarten. I tried to push that worry away and instead considered how much better the apartment looked and smelled now that everything was set up and the cabinets were stocked with staples. After dinner, I took Asher on his long-belated pilgrimage to the nearest playground.

I smelled a barbecue. Two men holding infants and two women sat around a picnic table outside an apartment. "Let's say hi to our neighbors." I took Asher's hand and walked toward them. "Do you all live here?"

One of the women looked at me warily. "More or less."

I extended my hand, introduced myself. "We just got here from Chicago."

I thought they would invite us to sit down, ask how old Asher was, what I was planning to study. Instead, the woman who'd spoken to me nodded toward one of the men, who cleared his throat and said, "Well, we're right in the middle of dinner."

"I'm sorry."

"Okay then." The dinner companions looked at one another, closed like the sides of a box and brought their conversation in tight.

We found a playground. There weren't any children playing there, and spider webs covered the equipment. I sat beneath a tree while Asher played. I pulled blades of grass, trying to keep them whole, feeling the smooth, stubborn glide of their roots separating from the earth.

"Watch, Mom," Asher called again and again. Each time, I was summoned to watch the same thing: Asher going up a ladder and down a slide.

"Good one, buddy!" I didn't mean it, but I made myself clap.

Late that night, after Asher was finally in bed, I made my way to my own room, wrapped myself beneath the bedcovers and turned off the lights.

"Mom?" Asher's voice sounded in the dark.

"You're supposed to be asleep." I hoped he would stay in his own bed. I would spend every minute of the next day with him. I thought I needed that night alone, as a buffer.

"I'm scared," he called from his bedroom.

"Good night." The plastic mattress sagged beneath my weight.

"But I'm scared."

"There's nothing to be scared of. Good night, Asher." I should have gotten up, sat with him, rubbed his back. I didn't move. Asher's breathing changed. His little-boy snores rang through the apartment. I didn't feel sorry that he'd gone to sleep without pity or comfort. Instead, I felt sorry for myself because two weeks would pass before Asher and I resumed the kind of schedules we'd maintained in Chicago. He wouldn't be in day care, and I had no idea how I'd pass the time.

Oregon's nights were darker than Chicago's. Pink false-dawn always lit Chicago's night skies. The noises were different there too. In Oregon, sounds of frogs and crickets replaced those of car-alarms and arguments. The loud frogs sounded menacingly nearby, and I wondered if one lived beneath my bed. I turned on the overhead light but was too afraid to look. I stared at the ceiling for comfort until I saw a large long-legged insect (later I would learn it was a crane fly) darting around the light fixture, its legs thudding heavily against the glass. I thought any flying bug that large would surely sting. I was too afraid I would miss it if I tried to take a swipe at it, that I would only make it angry. Finally, it found its way to the window screen. Trembling, I hurriedly closed the window, trapping the creature between screen and glass. Despite the heat, I wouldn't reopen the window until days later.

Other single mothers soon arrived at family housing. They unloaded cheap, used furniture and plastic toys from U-Hauls and the backs of cars. I remember feeling superior to them. I was a few years older, the only one in a graduate program rather than working towards a bachelor's degree and the only one, I learned quickly, who didn't receive food stamps. This, I felt, was the biggest difference between us. They weren't willing to work full time while they were in school and I was.

One afternoon, my son fell on the sidewalk and scraped his knee. He cried even though the knee didn't bleed or swell.

"You're fine," I told him. "Don't cry."

"Why don't you hug him?" my neighbor asked. She took Asher in her arms the way I'd often seen her take her own daughter, as if she would do anything to stop the child's pain. Asher leaned against her and his crying stopped. I had never held him like that, I realized. It never would have occurred to me. There was something missing in me, something broken. That night, Asher and I had the first real talk of our relationship. I lay down next to him, rubbed his back, and held him close. He told me that he wondered about his father. He told me he was scared to start school. He asked, "Do you hate me?"

"No," I said. "Of course I don't." I didn't ask him why he thought I did. I didn't want to know.

That was over a year ago. When school started, I didn't get a full-time job. I went to school and worked part time so I could be there for my son when he got home from kindergarten. Now, I am still in school, still working part time, still getting to know and love my son. We spend every afternoon, every evening, every weekend together. We go for nature walks, read and play, talk and hug. At dinnertime, he plays with my neighbors' kids while I cook with the other single mothers of my neighborhood. We all receive food stamps and pool those resources so that our kids can eat balanced, healthy meals every day. To some people, I know, my life sounds like a failure. Essentially, I went from work to welfare, the opposite of the culturally esteemed route. My child and I wear handed-down clothes and cheap shoes. We haven't got enough money to go out to dinner or the movies or to buy expensive toys. Sometimes I am so far behind on my bills that I receive more phone calls from creditors than from friends. I remind myself that even though I was better off financially before I moved to Oregon, I was fundamentally more impoverished because Asher and I were relatives, but not a family.

At the grocery store, I still feel ashamed as I hand the cashier my Oregon Trail card. I still hope that no one standing on line behind me can tell it's not a credit card. I consider again what the card signifies. Maybe it wasn't designed to exhort or to shame. Maybe, instead, it accurately reflects the simultaneous shame and pride of the nonindigenous American's story. We are more aware now of the costs of the Oregon Trail and the American Dream, the women and children who died along the way, the uprooting and destruction of native cultures. My pursuit of the American Dream, which ultimately led me to Oregon, also carried a grievous cost. It almost cost me a real relationship with my son. What I've accomplished in becoming a better mother is a different sort of dream. Perhaps it is a more universal human dream. I believe it is a triumph nonetheless.

Corrina Wycoff teaches English at Pierce College in Washington State. She has fiction and essays forthcoming in several places, including *Other Voices* magazine and an anthology, *The Clear Cut Future*, to be published by Clear Cut Press. She lives in Seattle with her son Asher, who is eight, and is working on a novel.

This essay was the winner of the 2001 *Oregon Quarterly* Northwest Perspectives Essay Contest. It appeared in the Summer 2001 issue of *Oregon Quarterly.*

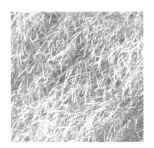

Train Time

Susan Rich

A lost elegance is reclaimed as train travel enjoys a resurgence in the Pacific Northwest.

I have fallen in love with trains. I've been seduced by their steady purr and tilting rhythms, by the long silver-nosed locomotive that threads itself like a needle through the night. I love to recite the names of the rail routes that traverse this state: the Coast Starlight and the Cascades. Perhaps most of all, I am enamored with the journey itself—train travel as a practiced art—with active participation by both customer and crew. Dining cars, boxed chocolates, the morning paper delivered by a well-dressed conductor. This romantic notion of the railroads may be at the heart of why train transportation in Oregon has been experiencing a comeback. Studies show that over the last five years, the number of people riding the trains between Eugene and Seattle has steadily increased. Since 1993, ridership has more than doubled, with more than half a million people traveling the Pacific Northwest corridor by train last year.

Initially, it was the coming of the railroad to the West that provided the impetus to construct bridges, cross rivers, tunnel through mountains of basalt. Physical barriers gave way to entrepreneurial and territorial dreams. Women designed new patchwork quilts to celebrate the train's arrival. One town held a "christening," while in others brass bands performed at the station to salute this new connection to a wider world. With the opening of the Shasta Route linking Oregon to California in 1887, the western states became accessible to outside markets—the movement of goods up and down the coast no longer dependent on an uncertain stagecoach ride. The railway removed the profound isolation of many small communities, and the people who lived there understood that their lives would never be quite the same. A headline in the *Oregonian* in 1884 proclaimed the railway as "an indispensable adjunct of civilization." Trains and all they promised—a boundless track, an irreversible economic and cultural transformation—may have sparked late-nineteenth-century imaginations in much the way personal computers and the World Wide Web represent the new frontier to us, travelers at the end of the twentieth century.

The morning is brisk and black at 4:45 A.M. as I switch off the alarm clock and fold a change of clothes into a small overnight pack. I've a ticket for Seattle on the 6:00 A.M. train departing from Eugene. Since the Cascades run originates here, the station master tells me, the train is guaranteed to leave on time. "If you arrive at 6:01," he warned me when I purchased my ticket the night before the trip, "you'll be waving good-bye to your seat from the platform." With his practiced charm and soft accent, I knew I could trust him. I arrive with ten minutes to spare and he smiles approvingly, remembering our conversation from the previous day.

As I climb the one step up to the train, despite the early hour, despite the familiar route I know we'll take, a certain visceral excitement catches me off guard. Call it a practiced mystery, the participation in a tradition that's been popular in Oregon for more than a hundred years—a pleasure trip that intersects with everyday life—but I can't board a train, grab the rails, without a rush of adrenaline, an irrational pleasure moving through my body before we even depart the station. I take note of the other passengers: a boy with the beginnings of a beard, a woman in black leather pants, an elderly couple holding hands. As we find our seats, remove our coats, I wonder, do they share this frisson, this seemingly innate appreciation for the ride?

The conductor who brings me the morning paper understands my fascination with trains. He explains that this morning's train-set is something special. Officially called a "Pendular Talgo" or more commonly known as a tilt train, the new technology works like a pendulum. The interaction between the suspension springs and the train's body allows each car to tilt naturally into the side of a curve while the wheels stay parallel to the tracks. These Talgo trains can travel speeds up to 125 miles-per-hour in ideal conditions and need not reduce speed for each separate hill or angle. When tracks on this run are repaired to properly handle them, these trains will shave sixty minutes off the Portland to Seattle route, making the trip from Union Station to King Street Station in two and a half hours. The Talgos, manufactured in Spain and shipped by sea to Seattle, are the first European-style cars to operate in regular service anywhere in North America.

Tilt trains began their official run in December 1998, arriving in a flurry of photo opportunities and press releases. The trains were christened in a gala ceremony in Seattle and news soon spread that the Mt. Baker and Mt. Rainier runs traveling to Eugene would now feature computer outlets, movies, telephones and Northwest cuisine. For this trip, I've been seduced by the ad campaigns to try the "Custom Class" option, which offers an extra-large seat, breakfast, Northwest coffee and the morning paper for only a few additional dollars. Ten dollars seems a reasonable price for a little luxury, especially compared to the exorbitance and extravagance of a first-class seat on an airplane, a privilege I've never been able to justify.

Susan Rich

Train travel in 1999 is a place to contemplate life rather than push against it, the journey a luxury for the spirit as much as for the body. Traveling by train allows for a certain space to be suspended out of time. Certainly we're aware of what time we should reach Portland or Olympia, but train time is marked differently than ordinary time. It is slower, more luxurious, it seems to pause between one moment and the next. We measure hours by the length of the rivers, the sight of familiar signposts. One couple I meet is completing a train ride from Albuquerque to Seattle. "We could have flown," Martha tells me, "but we wanted the train time to adjust to returning home. It just makes more psychic sense this way." In the Jewish tradition, the observance of the Sabbath emphasizes being in the moment, rather than in time. Like a train's arrivals and departures, the Sabbath's beginning and end take place at a precise moment. But like train time, that structure allows us to fully relax and experience what happens in between.

In 1860 when trains began their trek through Oregon, standard time zones did not exist. Nothing as strict as Central, Eastern, Mountain or Pacific time organized the country—or the globe. Each train could pass through dozens of different local time zones en route to its destination. Wisconsin, for example, had thirty-eight time zones, Michigan twenty-seven. In the 1880s, Union Pacific, which owned a section of track in Oregon (and still retains part ownership today), needed three different time clocks to operate. The Oregonian Railway Company rules and regulations included a policy for allowing five-minute delays at points where two lines converged to avoid problems caused by variations in train men's watches. Local time was determined from "high noon"—the point at which the sun hovered directly above the town center. Yet, how did Oregon find its time during winter months? The system was highly fallible, at best. Finally, in November 1883, after much debate it was decided that railroads would keep to four different time zones across the nation. Newspapers reported a large grassroots outcry; people protested that the new system was contrary to nature. "I keep God's time, not that of the railroads" was a common complaint. Each town with a railroad station eventually received a "regulator clock," strategically placed high on a tower adjoining the station, in clear view and safely out of reach of sabotage. Soon it became the fashion for gentlemen to set their pocket watches each morning by the tower clock. Time zones, time tables and train trips were inextricably linked.

It's 6:00 A.M., and the train pulls out of the Eugene station. The whistle trills through the morning sky like the notes of a harmonica, announcing our journey is beginning. Outside of town the electric lights appear as scattered pieces of gold and aquamarine, lost beads from the city's necklace. We pass the back sides of granaries, sacks fluffed and stacked in tight rows looking to all the world like eiderdown quilts, and industrial parks that appear in a quick flare of silver and smoke. Sometimes the train parallels the old highway for as much as a mile. I watch the red flash of Texaco stations and the traffic lights. Cars appear as white ghosts, headlights blurring the tarmac in the morning rain. We overtake them and speed again into landscape. Between the towns, trees begin to separate from their shadows, the sky turns from indigo to a spectral blue and again to a colorless light powder. "Breakfast is served," a voice announces, gently, over the loudspeaker. A few of us get up and move to the dining car.

Over omelets and orange juice, Elmira tells me that her husband worked for the rail yards for more than thirty years. Now a widow at eighty-one, she is on her way to Seattle to visit her sister and brother-in-law for the weekend. "My husband liked to take bus driver's holidays," she says with a laugh. With her bobbed white hair and Reeboks, she is an experienced traveler, having seen the entire West Coast by rail—from L.A. to Vancouver. Elmira has already read all about the Talgo trains and tells me that, in her opinion, high-tech trains have been a long time in coming.

Susan Rich

The first train-set built in the United States was finished in 1827. It ran three miles from the granite quarries of Quincy, Massachusetts, to the banks of the Neponsett River. In 1852, the first passenger train left Baltimore, Maryland, bound for Wheeling, West Virginia. Soon George Pullman in Chicago began amassing a business empire by converting day coaches into sleepers. Railroad fever was slowly edging its way westward. On May 10, 1869, the Golden Spike Ceremony celebrated the joining of the Union Pacific Railroad, building track west from Omaha, with the Central Pacific Railroad, moving east from Sacramento. Thousands of immigrant Irish and Chinese laborers worked to bridge, blast and tunnel their way through 1,800 miles of formidable terrain. The track connection in Utah was the final touch. The transcontinental railroad fell into place, shortening the previous six-month overland journey from New York to California to a matter of days. Ironically, the meeting of the tracks is also credited with being the first live, "on-line" event—the telegraph officer in Promontory Point, Utah, sending dots and dashes out across America, announcing the completion of the rails.

It's 8:00 A.M., and other passengers are beginning to stir, some of their faces creased from sleep. One woman sings to her daughter. Two teenage girls seated behind Elmira are enjoying an animated discussion about sex. Their coarse comments are interspersed with oohs and ahs as they break from their conversation and mark the scenery—the Willamette River tumbling high and fast to our left, a sheer rock face jutting far above the train's ceiling on the right. Across the aisle, a man wearing a red feather in his hat watches out his window as the riverscape changes within minutes to an industrial zone edged with towers holding natural gas. The motion of the train swings our car lightly, people's hips sway side to side as they walk through from the dining car on their way back to reclaim their seats.

"On time, Gary," the conductor says into his two-way radio. We arrive in Portland at 8:35 sharp. The red brick station with its adjoining clock tower holds shows more exciting than any theater. The ongoing series of interlocking dramas here are real: the implicit narrative of arrival, the freedom of departure, the station master's call for passengers headed to Centralia, Olympia, Vancouver—nothing of this scene has altered significantly during the last century. Even the old-style paintings on the station walls—large-scale renditions of the Shasta Route and the Cascade train-set racing past a snowcapped Mt. Hood—still hold currency in the traveler's imagination.

"The only way to catch a train on this road is to go with your blankets and a basket of grub and wait for the whistle; and you never want to buy a limited ticket, for if it doesn't expire before you get there, you will," advised Theodore Thurston Geer, Oregon's tenth governor, in an open letter to the *Oregonian* in 1887. Perhaps trains were not all the train companies purported them to be, at least in the early years of passenger travel. There were certainly long delays and, on occasion, robberies such as the infamous Tunnel 13 Bombing, a tragedy still spoken bitterly of today. On October 11, 1923, outside Siskiyou, near the California border, a train engineer was shot through the forehead, a fire-man killed, and a mail car exploded. Four years and a million dollars later, the three De Autremont brothers were captured in the biggest manhunt ever conducted in the state.

But trains are more than a page torn from history or folklore. Though they still have delays and occasional accidents, they have outlasted the stagecoach, made canal transport extinct, and may someday outlive the automobile as we know it. Today it is environmentally fashionable to hail trains as the antidote to overcrowded roads. The Coast Starlight and the Cascades are being reclaimed as elegant and energy-efficient modes of transportation. "Highways won't be able to meet our needs indefinitely," says Ken Skach Mills, president of the Association of Oregon Rail and Transit Advocates, a citizen action group that educates policymakers and the public about alternative transport. "The need for trains will only increase in the future."

It's 9:20 A.M., and we're on our way. On the video screens above our heads a map details our exact location, showing temperature and miles

Susan Rich

left until we reach our destination. The Global Positioning System, a constellation of satellites that provides precise location information, is tracking the train's every move. We cross the Willamette and then parallel the Columbia, where a single heron is fishing undisturbed by the metal drone. The landscape shifts from wild to human spaces: farmland and small shops. The train is passing homes: I see a woman putting on her jacket, stretching out her arms as we go by, a rocking horse in the backyard. We pass a golf course where men in white socks walk from hole to hole dragging their clubs. There are old clapboard houses with wrap-around porches and worn wooden fences. Silos and barns and horses dressed in blue cotton jackets. A certain pleasure comes from watching our world lumber across long stretches of spring grass, saunter by Holsteins sitting along a stream, roll past fir trees packed in like pencils as we sit back regally in our seats. In the rhythm of the rails we relax, talk with strangers, smile. Unlike the dejected bus atmosphere or the cold airplane stratosphere, the train trip inspires conversation, seats single passengers together in the dining car, encourages a mapping of the unexplored.

It's 10:32 A.M. and we're moving right through Winlock where the world's largest egg resides—a dirty white-colored orb elevated a hundred feet off the ground. Next is Evaline, where the schoolhouse built in 1883 is still in use. At 700 feet above sea level we've reached the highest point between our point of departure and our final destination. By now the conductor is singing his stops; Olympia becomes an aria. The music of the tracks may be his inspiration, for he's worked for Amtrak since the company began in 1976. The train leans into the curve as it turns towards Puget Sound. We're juxtaposed with mountains on one side and the opening to the sea on the other. We pass marinas with cruise ships and Navy patrol boats, islands, inlets and a confluence of minute streams.

Train lore, train songs, train love poetry. Walt Whitman called them "the pulse of the continent"; Emily Dickinson wrote "I like to see it lap the Miles—And lick the Valleys up—"; and Leadbelly sang "Let the Midnight Special shine its ever-lovin' light on me." Trains are an American icon. They conjure up a time when women wore white gloves to travel, and every man his best hat. Parlor cars with names like The Nugget had hand-carved trim and a silver cuspidor on the floor. You might be anyone going anywhere, but when you boarded a train like "The Daylight," "The Empire Builder," or "The Hercules," you held your head a bit higher and felt the brightness of the future inextricably linked with this sleek, speeding engine.

Passengers on the Cascades are making their way toward the lounge for a last drink before Seattle. The bartender performs a harmonica solo over the loudspeaker, signaling the last call at the Bistro Bar. We aren't served boxed chocolates or champagne as Seattle nears, as are the riders of trains that originate in Los Angeles. Still, this is much to savor as our journey is almost over. The scenery seems to move faster now: harbor lights in green neon, rows of red tractors, abandoned pumpkin patches, and fields of new spring seed. And to be honest, there are many spindles, and wires, and tubes I can't identify—the backstage of industry, a city-view I rarely see. People are pulling on their sweaters, re-buckling their bags. The rest of life is sneaking close again. Paul Gauguin, painting in a studio in Tahiti, scrawled on the border of one of his last works, "Where do we come from? Where are we going?" I think of that canvas, the luminous golds and the dark, brackish greens, and think that wherever it is we are heading, I will only agree to go if it's possible to arrive there by train.

Susan Rich is the author of *The Cartographer's Tongue: Poems of the World* (White Pine Press), winner of the PEN West Poetry award and the Peace Corps Writers award. Her poems have appeared in a number of publications, including the *Christian Science Monitor, DoubleTake, Harvard Magazine, Massachusetts Review* and *Poet Lore*. She teaches at Antioch University–LA in the MFA program and at Highline Community College in Seattle, Washington.

This essay appeared in the Summer 1999 issue of *Oregon Quarterly*.

Air, Earth, Fire, Water

Jane Kyle

Addressing the elements, one at a time.

The ancient philosopher Empedocles (490–430 B.C.), writing in the context of fifth-century B.C. Greek philosophy, described four primordial elements out of which everything in the cosmos is made. These are air, earth, water and fire. As to the mechanics of the cosmos, Empedocles proposed two forces which act on these four elements, calling them Love (Eros), which attracts and brings things together and which creates, and Strife (Polemos, also translated as Hate or Discord) which separates and destroys. Across time the cosmos unfolds with alternating periods of union and disunion, creation and destruction in a cyclical manner, that is, without end. The cosmos, according to Empedocles, is eternal. Our modern science, a veritable chalkboard of numbers and signs, is highly quantified by the standard of ancient philosophy. Yet even as the Nobel Prizes are handed out, we still find meaning in the simple metaphors of the old science. Things do come together, they do break apart, but still they persist in recombination. The idea of a perpetual cycle where chaos

113

repeats is at odds with our optimistic notion of progress, and yet faced with an intermittently cataclysmic natural world, we do well to stand back and take note.

I. Air

There are maybe twenty of us in the cabin of the jumbo jet, mostly airline representatives and Boeing employees and their kin. We are on the delivery flight of a new Boeing 747, departing Seattle, bound for Amsterdam, home city of KLM, the Royal Dutch airline. It's winter 1971. The folks who know each other from work congregate at the front of the plane and settle there once the pilot asks us to buckle up. I've been told the safest seat on an airplane is in the emergency exit row over the wing. That's where I go. The KLM rep is already seated there, strapping himself in. I take a window seat.

The 747 has the longest, slowest takeoff in the business. The engines don't roar and strain, the nose does not lurch up. Instead the plane ambles along, accelerating far too gradually, it seems, ever to break gravity. I concentrate on the sensations coming back to me from the plane: the droning of the engine, the slight vibration of rubber on tarmac, in order to pinpoint the moment of lift. There it is—we're flying! I'm idly watching the runway fall away below the wing, when the engine nearest my window blows out.

There's a flash—like a strobe—at the mouth of the engine and a small oblong panel flies off the side, an oddly silent catastrophe. In place of the bang I expect to hear, the KLM rep cries out, "My God!" It isn't the sound of a man in fear for his life, for unbelievably, the plane is not faltering, the airstrip is dwindling beneath us, we are seemingly on our way. The other passengers wouldn't guess we are flying on three engines instead of four. I don't know why the Number Three shut down, but the KLM rep has his theory. He leans toward me. "A bird," he says. "We took in a bird." I look at him, disbelieving.

The captain will confirm this over the intercom within minutes. We're going back to land. But first we jettison fuel, circling west towards the

Olympic Mountains then back over Puget Sound. As the plane banks and turns in a wide square I see picture-perfect views of greater Seattle beneath the broken engine: the islands, the hills, the inland lakes, the skyscrapers, Alki Point where I used to go wading as a kid. A veil of jet fuel streams away behind us, ungracing the lovely setting. The KLM rep is telling me the bird problem at the Amsterdam airport is the worst in all aviation and they've resorted to shooting blanks to flush the birds. "Ya," he is saying, "the plane has to wait on the runway for the bird patrol to go first. Two guys in a jeep. One drives, the other stands up and shoots. The birds take off. But they come back." Then, looking sorrowful, the rep tells me KLM will have to pay Boeing outright to replace the exploded engine. "One million dollars," he says. "No warranty for birds."

I look out the window to the second engine now doing the work of the pair. I look down at the land, tilting beneath us. My father, an engineer, once drew me a picture of an airplane wing with curving arrows representing the wind gliding over its curved top, but with swirling arrows underneath the wing representing the principle of lift. Then, as if not trusting the diagram to be graphic enough for his daughter, he curved his right hand over his left fist and thrust the right hand skyward at a takeoff angle. "Air lifts," he said. "It lifts under the wing." As I float above Seattle, I remember this science as if it were a promise from home, and yet I still can't turn my mind from the image of a posse in a jeep and a marksman hanging on for life and shooting into the wind, while the perennial birds rise and scatter, every takeoff a narrow escape.

II. Earth

At the University of Washington, spring quarter 1965, I take Introductory Geology from a young professor who wrote the book on the geology of the Cascades. Although we are all beginners in his field and sit staring down at him from the concrete risers of a dimly-lit lecture hall, he talks easily in everyday tones, as if we were face to face, as if there were nothing difficult about his science that a good storyteller could not get across to undergraduates, no matter their major.

Over the weeks, we learn to identify types of rock and to read a rockbed from top to bottom. We learn to spot a tilted stratum and a faultline. Soon we have enough evidence to understand geology in a piecemeal, regional way. Then our professor asks us to think about the whole of geology—all the formations on all the continents and even the formations under the sea. He tells us his science is just beginning to formulate a unified theory that will explain, say, not just how a volcano works but why it's there at all. The master mechanism he proposes is called plate tectonics. As it turns out, it has taken the science of geology as long to get to this theory as it has taken us to settle the American West and, conveniently for him, the evidence of the Cascades, a volcanically active mountain range on America's West Coast, is a part of the puzzle that locks the theory in place on the continent.

Plate tectonics describes the earth as a molten core upon which a hardened crust floats. The crust fractures along a sequence of faults, the way mud drying in a lakebed cracks into patches. The surface of the planet is a totality of patches or plates, moving imperceptibly over the molten core, groaning against each other, some riding up over others, others being forced downward, compressed by incalculable forces. Plate tectonics is the best explanation we have for the origin of the great cordillera running from Alaska to Tierra del Fuego. Such mountain ranges are the crumple of a slow-motion collision of one plate over the top of another.

The theory of plate tectonics also accounts for other facts of West Coast life. One is volcanism. Compression makes rock hot, and hot rock seethes and flows. The other is earthquakes. Plates rubbing against one another compress for a time and seem to stick, until enough force builds, whereupon they jolt—and we fall down.

Our professor is talking to the class about earthquakes: "We do know about where they will happen. We think we know why. We can say an earthquake is bound to happen at such and such a time. But we can't say exactly when. Besides, what would you do if I told you there would be an earthquake on Monday?" He pauses for effect. He's used this line before. "Move to Miami Beach?" We laugh. The bell rings. It's Friday.

On Monday morning, I am taking a sociology quiz in one of the old buildings on the Quadrangle. There begins a roaring, like a steam train bearing down, except you can't locate the coming and going. The ground shimmies, so little at first I think it's just my own dizzy spell, but then this accelerates and deepens until the floor begins to slide and the walls to rock. When I was a kid in school during the Cold War, we drilled once a month for civil defense, scurrying under the windows when the teacher called up a nuclear blast, but under the tables when she called up an earthquake. On this Monday in sociology class, I remember those drills in a slow motion flashback, but it's ten strides to the hall, ten strides to the outside and I run. The bricks rattling over the entrance do not fall on me and I stay on my feet down the stairs.

At 6.5 on the Richter scale, the quake is a proverbial big one, but, fortunately, not a long one. Area-wide seven die, three from falling debris, four from heart failure. Damage is counted in dollars at 12.5 million. But this writing down numbers after the fact does not tell how an earthquake shakes the living. Before, we have bedrock and a place to pile our assumptions. After, we have slurry and dust, not easy metaphors for the grounding.

At the first geology class after the earthquake, we wait for the young professor. As he strides to the podium, we clap, and then we stand and cheer and stomp the floor. The professor bends at the waist, making a little bow. Then he holds out his hands, palms up, tips his head to one shoulder, and grins.

III. Fire

On the morning of May 18, 1980, Mount Saint Helens explodes into plumes of superheated ash. The top quarter of the mountain, a nearly perfect triangle that once gave the volcano a postcard silhouette, is gone in a flash, blasted into powder with the force of many atom bombs. The ash sears the land and smothers campers in their tents. Some men working on the mountain see the ash coming, leap for the pickup and drive like hell down the narrow Forest Service roads. Others try to outrun the

Jane Kyle

horror on foot but are overcome. The fire in the belly of the earth has come to ground.

To the east of the mountain ash rains down on Wenatchee, Washington, obscuring the daylight. In Portland the ash comes down on us in a dry drizzle. It is grainy, like borax from the sky. The ash powders your bare arms, dusts your hair, and gets between your teeth. When you bite down, there is a grittiness, like the aftermath of eating clams you haven't taken much care to rinse first before cooking. You expect sand in clams. You don't expect it from the sky.

The falling ash makes the day seem gloomy and casts a pall, the way a dreary stretch of weather does, although we aren't experiencing weather as such—and this is confounding. Announcers on the news tell us not to drive. Ash will grind up the engine, they warn. They tell us not to wipe the car. This will scratch the paint. They tell us to clear our gutters before the first rain.

I get out my ladder, set it against our house and climb up to have a look. Gutters, deep with ash. I take a fistful down to my husband, who once braved the summit of the mountain in a near whiteout.

"Look," I say. "Mount Saint Helens is in our gutters."

Holding the ash out to him in my open hand, I say, "Maybe you walked on this part. Now here it is."

IV. Water

We are several dozen fifth-graders on a field trip, and we are cold and hungry, because it is January in the Pacific Northwest and they have made us ride all morning in a school bus to get to the fish hatchery and now they are making us tour the place before we can have our lunch. It's damp inside the hatchery and the air is as cold as the mountain spring they channel inside to incubate the fish. We are all cranky as the tour guide leads us to the concrete rim of an in-ground tank and invites us to peer over. The grumbling stops.

A million silver fingerlings shimmer through the gloomy water. There is something compelling in the hectic flashing back and forth of the proto-fish. We are the young of our species looking in on the young of another, moved by that sudden curiosity which makes kids mature in the moment and ripe to learn. But the guide is talking down to us. He calls the adult salmon "mother salmon" and "father salmon" and their offspring "baby salmon." He tells us that salmon come from eggs, that they hatch in the water, that they eat a lot and, like us, they grow big. He tells us that baby salmon are born in streams like the one outside the hatchery, but then migrate a long, long way to sea. He says that two adult salmon have to make many, many babies. I wait for him to tell us that's because lots of them die before they make it downstream, but he must think this will upset us. So he turns to the story of the homecoming instead. When the grownup salmon are ready to lay more eggs, he says, they swim out of the sea, into the rivers and streams and all the way back to where they were born. They never get it wrong. They always find home. It's really hard work to get up the stream, though, and the salmon get very, very tired along the way. After they lay their eggs, they go to sleep and die.

He shows us photographs. The saddest one is where the old fish look so beaten up. The most amazing one is where the fish fight their way up falling water. In one picture, a large salmon is suspended in the air above the slanting water, its head pointed upstream. The body of the salmon is convulsed. The guide tells us the salmon is navigating a fish ladder. The word *ladder* is comforting in the face of the frank photographs. People climb ladders to get over things. Now fish can, too. Yes, the guide is saying in so many words. Dams are no problem. People think of everything. Look how we make it easy for fish. We kids are proud to live in salmon country where the fish work so hard and people help them out. Then it's time for lunch.

On another January morning almost fifty years later, I go jogging near Sammammish Slough in Redmond, Washington. This town is home to Microsoft, the high tech company that's replaced Boeing in America's mind as the business from Seattle. High tech is said to be easier on the earth.

It's six-thirty as I leave the house and it won't be light for another half hour. Just before going out, I hear a report on the radio about the energy crisis in California where there have been rolling blackouts all through the week. The radio announcer says the whole of the West Coast may soon be in trouble. Oregon and Washington traditionally sell hydropower to California in the winter and California returns the favor in the summer. The power trade works so long as either partner has a surplus. This winter, because of an uncharacteristic lack of rain in the Pacific Northwest, we have nothing to spare.

On the radio, a pleasant female reporter interviews an earnest male naturalist from Washington State about the impact of low water levels in this year of scarce rainfall. It would be possible, he is explaining, to draw down Northwest rivers in order to generate surplus electricity for California, but this will further threaten the fishery, leaving fish nowhere to swim. The salmon are already endangered, he is telling us. In fact, the salmon we remember are nearly gone.

As I jog along the Sammammish Slough that January morning, I pass a large wooden sign board describing how volunteers are restoring habitat on the waterway which was once upon a time a spawning ground for fish. The sign is lit through the night, although no one walks this path in the dark. I turn off the walkway towards the new upscale development that runs a half mile down the slough. I go past successive townhouses, each cluster feigning a village, with names like Windwood and Rivertrail, each of them lit blazingly while their inhabitants sleep. At the end of the road, I come upon Avignon, with its Mediterranean style so out of keeping with the woodsy theme. The water in the Avignon swimming pool glows turquoise from underwater lighting and the deck area is ablaze. Adjacent to the pool, a gazebo covers a fountain where a constant flow of water, driven by an electric pump round the clock, bubbles over a terra cotta basin into a holding pool. A marketing refrain for a readymade Eden. Live here, the soothing water whispers, live here with us, you want to live here.

Jane Kyle has won awards for teaching, writing and captaining a team of women in the relay from Mount Hood atop the Oregon Cascades to Pacific City on the coast. She teaches in the Performing and Fine Arts department at the University of Portland.

This essay was the second-place winner in the 2001 *Oregon Quarterly* Northwest Perspectives Essay Contest.

I Love the Rain

Lauren Kessler

Sodden clouds, intermittent wipers and home.

I love the rain.

I don't mean I grudgingly appreciate its ecological necessity. I don't mean I've learned to tolerate it. I don't mean I wait it out, flipping through the calendar to see how many more pages until the sun might break through. I mean I *love* it.

I love everything about it. I love falling asleep under a down comforter in the dead of winter with the windows thrown open to the hiss of rain. I love waking up to the soft aqueous light that is a painter's dream and listening to the rush of water in the culvert. I love the thrum of rain against the house on a dark afternoon with potato leek soup simmering on the stove. I love the fine mist on my face, the way my skin feels soft and pliant and new in the rain. I love thinking of words to describe the thick, sodden sky: pearl gray, dove gray, iron gray, pewter, ashen, silver, smoke. I love my big, green, knee-high Wellies. I love the intermittent wipers on my car.

But it was not always so.

The first winter I spent in western Oregon was the second wettest winter in recorded history, or so I was told. It started raining October first and by Halloween, the *Register-Guard* was running out of meteorological bon mots to print by the side of the masthead. I cut out the one that said "the wet stuff again" and sent it to my parents in New York, where, despite other notorious regional failings, it seems to know when to rain and when to stop.

At first, I found the rain enchanting. It seemed to make everything greener than it already was, and green was why I was in Oregon, so greener was better. That thought sustained me for perhaps a week, which was probably the longest continuously soggy period I had ever experienced.

But very soon the rain became an annoyance. The beautiful, old, crumbling house I was living in began to leak at the seams. Rain inched in under the back door. Puddles collected on the windowsills in the kitchen. The bathroom ceiling began to weep. Mostly I stayed inside and thought about how lovely San Francisco was this time of year. When I ventured out, I walked with chin tucked, shoulders hunched, eyes downcast. I winced a lot, as if every raindrop left an indentation in my skin. It was Thanksgiving by then, and it had been raining, unabated, for fifty-six days.

I scanned the *Guinness Book of World Records* for climatic catastrophes to make myself feel better: the longest drought (China), the largest hailstones (South Dakota), the worst mudslides (Southern California). I had lived through five Chicago winters, during which sheets of ice formed on the insides of my apartment windows and my socks froze inside my boots. I had weathered several hurricanes, one of which tore off most of the roof of my parents' house. One summer when I was working in central Minnesota, I watched from the tiny basement window of a bank as a full-blown tornado spiraled down Main Street. Surely I could live through this. It was then just before Christmas. It had been raining for all or part of seventy-nine days.

The sky seemed low enough to touch. Some mornings I thought the clouds would smother me. I became obsessed with seeing the sun. One (rainy) day after New Years, I borrowed a friend's car. "I'm going to drive east until it stops raining," I told him. I thought I might have to drive hundreds of miles, a thousand miles, maybe, back to the hard, cold Midwest where the trees were bare, and the wind was punishing, but the winter skies were often cobalt blue. As it turned out, all I had to do was get over the Cascades. I knew little about Oregon geography back then and had no idea relief was so close at hand. After a few days in Bend, I returned a slightly saner person.

Several months later, I left the Northwest for a job in downstate Illinois, where I was prepared to enjoy a long, crisp autumn followed by a cold, bright winter segueing into an ever-so-slightly showery but otherwise lovely spring. At least that was the plan.

The weather cooperated all right, but I hadn't counted on something: I missed Oregon. I missed hiking up Spencer Butte through the damp, ferny forest. I missed swimming in the icy waters of Little Fall Creek. I missed those mornings on campus when the air was thick with the yeasty smell of bread fresh from the ovens at Williams Bakery.

And, unbelievably, I missed the rain. There was something about the soft flannely light, the smell of rain-washed air, the peaceful tedium of long, wet days that drove you not just inside the house but inside yourself. I was, I told my friends, "homesick." I had spent barely more than a year in Oregon, but now, too late and two thousand miles away, I realized it was home.

I listened to the Joni Mitchell song that goes "you don't know what you've got 'til it's gone" so often that it played in my head even when it wasn't playing on the turntable. I read *Another Roadside Attraction*, savoring the over-the-top, rain-drenched prose. I read the journals of Lewis and Clark, noting that their winter at Fort Clatsop was not unlike my winter in Eugene. I read and then re-read *Sometimes a Great Notion*. And, a year later, when a bad opportunity came knocking—the wrong job for a lousy salary (no, not the job I have now)—I jumped at it because it would bring me back to Oregon.

Lauren Kessler

That was twenty-five years ago. I haven't been seriously tempted to leave since.

Now it's those hot, dry August days that drive me crazy, the sky bleached white around the edges, oak leaves brittle on the trees, pavement that burns feet through sandals, that big, bright, unrelenting, energy-sapping sun. I take down the calendar and leaf through the pages. If I'm lucky this year, only one more month until the rains come.

Lauren Kessler is the author of ten books, including *Clever Girl: Elizabeth Bentley and the Dawn of the McCarthy Era* (HarperCollins, 2003), Los Angeles *Times* bestseller *The Happy Bottom Riding Club* (Random House, 2000) and Oregon Book Award-winning *Stubborn Twig* (Random House, 1993). She directs the literary nonfiction program at the School of Journalism and Communication at the University of Oregon.

This essay appeared in the Winter 2001 issue of *Oregon Quarterly.*

Accelerate. Focus. Explode.

Cynthia Pappas

A team of women find synchronicity in the water.

In the boathouse, the coxswain calls out, "Hands on, ready and lift, up to shoulders, walk it out." The deceptive weight of this svelte-looking shell forces us to sway until we can steady our knees and lock our elbows with the boat overhead. The coxswain bellows, "Roll to waist, ready and down." Miraculously, the shell lands in the water right side up and none of us falls in.

We step gingerly into the tipping two-foot-wide shell. "Count down from bow when ready!" Her voice brings us back to the task at hand. We push off from the dock. It is our first row together as a team. We balance the sixty-foot-long shell on the still water as we make our way across Dexter Reservoir, twenty miles southeast of Eugene, Oregon.

Our goal: Compete in the Frostbite Regatta at Green Lake, Washington, in November. It is mid-July; only sixteen weeks to will our bodies into racing form.

I am assigned a starboard oar, bow position. At the coxswain's command, "Ready, row," we slide back, arms pulling blades through the water. For a moment we stroke together in a discordant rhythm, gliding across the water as one. It's a powerful feeling.

I'm hooked.

The team—Oregon Association of Rowers (O.A.R.)—is made up of eight women and our male coach. Our average age is forty-two.

Six weeks later, we push off from the dock as the sun breaks over the hills to the east. The bow four still struggle, though the stern four look pretty good. We practice catch drills, so our oars will all enter the water at the same time, making our strokes more efficient. Slowly we learn this intricate dance involved in becoming a team.

We row the distance of our race—1,000 meters—four times. The only sound is the creak of the riggers and the plop of the blades as they enter the water. Coach Craig hovers alongside in the motorboat, barking commands. "Catch together. Fast hands away. Use your legs. Put some power into it." Our fastest time is four minutes, twenty seconds—far longer than our three-minute, fifty-second goal. Hugely satisfying, nevertheless.

It's the first time in my life I admit out loud: I am competitive. I have spent so long throttling my ambition; now I want my team to see the whole me. Rowing makes me feel more alive. While scrubbing myself in the shower, I notice biceps that could win at arm wrestling. Hamstrings that are boxy and hard. I have muscles.

Nine weeks to race day. Full moon and the water is smooth as silk. A wonderful row this evening, almost Zen-like. Just two days later, however, a litany of admonitions runs through my head during the entire workout: Reach farther forward on your catch. Faster hands at the finish.

The act of rowing takes intense, whole-body concentration. Drive backward with thigh and calf muscles. Squeeze the oar into the stomach. Once in the finish position, bend forward from the waist before bringing the knees up into a forward slide. Catch, drive, finish, slide. Focus.

We seek perfect synchronization, blades moving in continuous, fluid motion. When all eight oars catch together, all you can hear is *cha*. The sound of mastery. It is the ultimate team sport. Eight women step into the boat as one body. Catch together. Hands away together. Swing in unison. Slide together.

I have never been athletic. At twenty-one, I played my first sport—racquetball. Now, at forty-one, I'm on a team of rowers; we've hired a coach and will compete in a sanctioned race in another state. How did this happen?

Three weeks until race day: We practice race starts. Brief, breathless strokes get the boat moving from a standstill to thirty strokes per minute within the first fifty feet of the race. The coxswain chants like an auctioneer, "Sit ready. Ready. Row."

Then we practice power tens. We push back so hard with our thigh and calf muscles that we rise up out of our seats. Now I understand why our shoes are bolted into the boat.

At home I make subtle adjustments in my lifestyle to ensure that I will be whole on race day. The night before workouts I go to bed early. I wake up at 6:30 A.M. to stretch, eat something, digest, then drive to the lake. Where is the person who used to sleep in on weekends?

One week from race day—our last practice. At Dexter, the water moves in half-foot-high rollers, coming up through the dock like something alive. The fall wind ices in toward shore. Everything is glassy, brilliant and fresh. Our coxswain manages to push us to a four-minute, six-second time.

November 13, 1999. Race day. 1:00 P.M.: It is overcast and misting heavily, but the water is smooth. A perfect day for racing. 2:00 P.M.: Coach gives our pre-race pep talk. "This is it. You can do this. You're athletes."

The race official confirms the starting line. "Lake Union, Kenai, U of O, Alaska, O.A.R." My stomach is in a knot. The race aligner calls out, "O.A.R. hold your position." Our coxswain says, "Sit ready."

The race official bellows, "Attention. Go." And just like that, the race begins.

Our start is incredible. The cox yells, "Your rate is thirty-six!" Faster than we have ever started. We move out in front of the other four boats.

Cynthia Pappas

"Power ten," she commands. We stay even with the UO team in lane three. We surge past the Kenai crew.

"Accelerate! . . . Focus! . . . Explode!" I can't tell where we are. Have we passed the 800-meter buoy? Are we in the final sprint? Cheers from the dock grow louder. The horn goes off. We cross the finish line. Two boats remain on the water. We've come in third. Ten seconds behind the UO boat—rower's average age: twenty.

We are athletes.

▪

Cynthia Pappas is the development services director for the city of Springfield, Oregon.

This essay appeared in the Spring 2000 issue of *Oregon Quarterly.*

Take Me Out to the Ballgame

Guy Maynard, Robert Leo Heilman, Robin Cody
& Joni James

*Nine players spread across an open field, each with a
distinct space and role. A batter trying to put rounded
wood to moving ball. Each player with an even chance
of being hero or goat. An almost perfect tension of
individual performance and collective result.*

Baseball. Precious moments in small places and grand events that stand
as signatures of their time. An unpredictable but inexorable rhythm of
work and rest, of stillness and motion, of silence and the pop of a fastball
in a catcher's mitt, the sudden rap of a solid hit, or the roar of a rising
crowd of fathers and sons and mothers and daughters and neighbors and
friends.

Baseball was never just a kid's game, though kids love it best. And it is
not just the multi-zillion-dollar entertainment industry of the George
Steinbrenners and Albert Belles.

Baseball is a game, a wonderful game of great skill and excitement, for
both players and fans. But it is a game that reaches deeper than any other
into the psyche of America and Americans. "…the one constant through
all the years has been baseball," writes W.P. Kinsella in his marvelous book
Shoeless Joe, which provided the basis for the movie *Field of Dreams.*
"America has been erased like a blackboard, only to be rebuilt and erased

131

again. But baseball has marked time while America has rolled by like a procession of steamrollers.... It is a living part of history, like calico dresses, stone crockery and threshing crews eating at outdoor tables. It continually reminds us of what once was, like an Indian-head penny in a handful of new coins."

If baseball can no longer claim to be our national pastime, if it is losing the rating wars—not just on television, but also on the more important sand lots and school fields—to the faster, action-packed spectacles of football and basketball, perhaps that as well as any other social barometer can tell us how we have changed as we head into the twenty-first century.

But they still love baseball in Roseburg, Oregon.

Eight teams from throughout the United States traveled to Roseburg last August to take part in the American Legion World Series (ALWS). American Legion baseball is for boys up to eighteen years old, usually the best high school players in an area. There are 4,791 Legion teams in the United States, including 109 in Oregon. The eight teams that made it to the ALWS—Yardley, Pennsylvania; Rockland County, New York; Gonzales, Louisiana; Midland, Michigan; Rowan County, North Carolina; Sandy, Utah; Rapid City, South Dakota; and Vancouver, Washington—had played anywhere from forty-five to eighty-eight games and won state and regional playoffs before coming to Roseburg.

Yardley won. They beat Gonzales—a talented, spirited team that became the favorite of the Roseburg crowd—in a tense championship game that turned on a single two-out, two-strike pitch* in the seventh inning. To most of the crowd the pitch looked like it should have been called strike three, ending the inning. The umpire saw it differently, called that pitch a ball. That batter eventually walked, the inning continued and Yardley scored the runs that gave them the lead and, two innings later, the game. Baseball is like that. Yardley wasn't a very impressive-looking team

---

*The losing pitcher that night, young Ben Sheets of the Gonzales team, went on to pitch, and win, the gold medal game for Team USA in the 2000 Olympic Games in Sydney, Australia. Sheets now pitches for the major league Milwaukee Brewers.

and had no memorable stars. In the awards ceremony after the game, Gonzales players got most of the individual honors. Yardley just got the great big championship trophy. Baseball is like that, too.

More than 35,000 fans showed up for the five-day tournament, breaking the attendance record, which was set in 1993, the last time the ALWS was held in Roseburg. Among those 35,000 were three Oregon writers (one would now be more accurately labeled a former Oregon writer) who have a special place in their hearts for baseball and all that it touches.

—*Guy Maynard*

Old Boys

Bill Harper, a scout for the Phillies, is missing out on Saturday's noon game, sitting across the street at a picnic table in the park. Later, he'll be back in his front-row seat behind home plate, in time to watch the last five innings and earn his honest pay with a scouting report. But for now, he's got something more important to do—a meeting with some boys who are now grandfathers, some ballplayers he hasn't seen in half a lifetime.

Roseburg's 1956 Umpqua Post #16 team is holding their first reunion. Forty years ago, Bill Harper was their manager and they were one of four teams competing in the American Legion World Series in Bismarck, North Dakota. Since then, thirteen teams from Oregon have made it that far. But they were the first, a Cinderella team from a sawdust town in the middle of nowhere.

The picnic is just beginning, but already over half the team is there—Bill Harper and his former coach, Don Severson; the mostly pot bellied and graying boys who played for them; wives, children, grandchildren. The men treat Harper with a lingering deference—not exactly formal but with a trace of awe—as they introduce him to their families. Harper seems a bit shy and bemused.

"You know," he says later, back at the stadium, "I think I learned more about those guys in forty-five minutes over there this afternoon than I did the whole time I coached them."

The core of the team came from Glide, a small mill town east of Roseburg on the North Umpqua River. Tiny Glide High School took the state baseball championship in 1956, thanks largely to the pitching of Dick Smith and his cousin, Allen Smith.

The stories go 'round, about Dick Smith's uncanny adolescent accuracy in spitting, the rattler they killed at a roadside stop near Bend, barf bags on the first airplane ride any of them had ever taken. It's obvious they can't ever forget what they went through together.

There's a closeness to these men on the cusp of retirement, an appreciative understanding and fond regard that shows in their eyes, in their smiles, in the tone of their voices as they josh each other, like old campaigners at a military unit reunion. They speak in the same sort of personal code, the names of towns and cities—Yakima, The Dalles, Billings, Bismarck—calling up long-gone hotel rooms and cafes, ball parks, line drives and double plays, the mood and feel and texture of those brief weeks when they felt invincible, when adversity just made them tougher to beat.

They weren't expected to win the state championship that year, let alone fight their way through the playoffs all the way to Bismarck. The extra weeks on the road were more than the team could afford. Dick Smith's dad lost his lumber mill job by sticking with the team. Rob Beamer saved thirty-two silver dollars from his five-dollars-per-day meal money to help his parents pay for gas. His old first baseman's glove disintegrated in Billings and the local Legion post bought him a new one.

Mac McClellan's squeeze bunt scored the winning run in pitcher Bill Oerding's game in Billings and sent them on to the World Series. Oerding's mother died from a heart attack that hit her in the stands that night. He went on to Bismarck anyway because "that's what she would have wanted." There he pitched against Yonkers, New York, winning eight-to-five, and earned the first Sportsmanship Award in Legion World Series history.

Umpqua took third place in that year's four-team tournament and went home to a statewide celebration. Governor Mark Hatfield congratulated them. The mayor of Portland handed them the key to the city. Their team bus was waylaid outside of Roseburg and the boys rode in a string of new Thunderbird convertibles, down hometown streets temporarily renamed in their honor and out to their Roseburg High School home field where 3,000 people waited in the stands to cheer them.

It was John Livingston, athletic director at Glide High School, a reserve outfielder in 1956 and the youngest member of the team, who noticed the convergence of a fortieth anniversary and this year's series in Roseburg. He looks back over the years and at the faces around him. He's seen a lot—as a centerfielder for the University of Oregon, as a minor league player with the Twins, as a PE teacher and coach at Glide High School and as a Legion coach with the 1984 Umpqua Post #16 team that went to the Legion World Series in New Orleans.

"You know," he says, "it really gets me when school boards talk about cutting budgets for athletics—as if these programs were unimportant."

The 1956 Roseburg team is introduced to the crowd before Sunday morning's game. One by one they trot out on the field and line up on the grass behind home plate, at first a little shyly, but as the line of potbellied men grows longer their high-fives grow exuberant. Nearly the entire team is here—twelve of the fifteen players, along with manager Harper and coach Severson and Gordon Smith, a frail old man who was sponsor of the team. Only the batboy and two surviving members of the team are missing.

Their enthusiasm is infectious. Many of the spectators at this loser's bracket game are men with decades of involvement in amateur baseball—as players, coaches, umpires, high school athletic directors, league presidents and commissioners. The applause gets louder and rowdier with each introduction. The reunited team basks, once again, in the applause. They deserve it. Their one season forty years ago generated the excitement that led to the building of this stadium and to the community support that brought this tournament here.

But what about the young men from far away who have come to play this game. Kids these days, could they understand something like this? Does the sight of these old guys trotting out on the field fill them with inspiration or remind them of their own mortality? Does it mean a damn thing to them?

Over on the first-base side, Rapid City, South Dakota's players are slouching on their bench, fiddling with equipment, talking, sipping Gatorade and waiting for their own introduction, the recitation of the Code of Sportsmanship, the National Anthem and the game. Opposite them, the Athletic Club from Gonzales, Louisiana, is lined up on the top step of their dugout, clapping politely at first and then, catching the crowd's joy, smiling and applauding with what can only be described as genuine enthusiasm.

The old guys pose for a team photo, turn around to face the field and take part in the rest of the opening ceremony. Finally they shuffle off to the stands where they sit together to watch the game before they split up and head their separate ways back home.

—*Robert Leo Heilman*

Home and Away

A middle-sized town throwing a major league party needs a gung-ho organizer, someone to motivate volunteers, wheedle a donation here, kick a butt there, juggle four balls at once and keep smiling.

"My home is this ball field," says Helen Lesh. "They put my phone number on the Internet. I get more phone calls than President Clinton." Lesh, seventy-three, with fluffy white hair, piercing blue eyes and an air of unchallenged authority, rules from her command post behind the grandstand. Officially, she is in charge of ticket sales, souvenirs and concessions. Unofficially, she is the Energizer Bunny for crisis management. If

Lesh can't solve your problem, she knows who can. *Ask Helen* is the emergency response phrase here, the equivalent of *call 911* in the big city.

Like amateur baseball itself, volunteerism is more central to life in Roseburg than to life in Portland or Eugene. The service ethic here is all about connections. "When I call up a businessman," says Lesh, "he knows me." That business person also knows that a donation of time or money will be noticed by others in a position to give. These people are neighbors. Giving begets giving. A single focal point—American Legion baseball—becomes a source of huge community pride. And Lesh can fire up volunteers because she works harder for no pay than anybody.

"Helen phoned me at 7:30 this morning," says Tom Donegan of the Lions Club. "She said, 'I hope I didn't wake you up. But you should be up anyway.'"

When Lesh needs a cover photo for the World Series program, she has a friend bring his airplane in for an aerial shot of the field. Screening concessionaires, she rejects commercial applicants and awards booths to local service clubs. Profits stay in Douglas County. Because she knows the governor (Lesh ran the Bloodmobile when Kitzhaber ran the local emergency room), John promptly returns her call, and Helen tells him what to say by way of a welcome-to-Oregon message in the program.

While Lesh is the sergeant-major, attending to details, her husband Ralph shares generalship of the 1996 ALWS with Bill Gray, longtime champion of Roseburg baseball. Gray and other civic leaders have poured years of volunteer labor and materials-at-cost into what is now, by far, the finest amateur baseball grounds in Oregon. The coach from Louisiana—on his first look at the immaculate field, covered grandstands, freshly painted scoreboard, spanking-new dugouts and lights—caught his breath and asked, "Who plays here?" Thinking it had to be a professional team, he was astounded to learn it was a home field for Legion ball.

"Baseball is a boost for the economy," says Mike Winters, a county commissioner manning a rake on the grounds crew. "The visitors stay in Roseburg motels. They rent cars and drive to the coast, to Crater Lake. They'll go back and tell people about Douglas County."

Lesh, too, has her eye on business. Her earnings—from selling T-shirts, buttons and seat cushions—go straight to the baseball program. After a banker doubted that she deserved a charge card scanner, Lesh got indignant and showed him gross receipts of $40,000 from the 1993 ALWS. "We're doing even better this time," she says.

If given free rein, Lesh would do too much herself. Gray, recently on the phone with her, was put on hold while she gave the Corvallis newspaper a report on the series. When she came back on the line, he had to remind her about her volunteer duties, which did not include those of press officer. But the lady sees something to be done, and she does it. Gray's only real worry is that she might wear herself out. "Oh, I won't wear out," she says. "I might pass away, but I won't get tired."

Busy during the series with sales and troubleshooting, Lesh doesn't get to see the games. "I never saw a pitch in the '93 series," she says. "The only time I went to the stands was when that lady had a heart attack in front of my booth." Lesh had sold the cardiologist his tickets. She knew right where the doctor was sitting, so she hustled out and got him.

This year, again, Lesh didn't see a pitch. But at the closing ceremony, the Legion moguls hauled her onto the infield grass, under the bright lights, where local fans gave her a rousing ovation. Lesh, speechless, didn't know what all the fuss was about. The people of Roseburg knew. Her neighbors knew that Helen Lesh is what community is, and what big cities are missing.

If you were searching the other side of America for the mirror image of Douglas County, you'd stop at Rowan County, North Carolina. The population center is Salisbury, a Roseburg-sized city, and the Legion team draws also from small towns similar to Oregon's Myrtle Creek, Winston and Glide. Rowan County is soy bean and tobacco farm country, and many of the ball players come from no town at all. The accents are different, but the common language is baseball—with all its attendant dreams.

The Rowan County nine swept its regional tournament in five games. Just two days later they find themselves 3,000 miles from home, lined up for the national anthem at the opening game of the ALWS. It's 9:30 A.M. Fifty state flags hang limp in the blue air above a field where every blade of grass has its place and every ball player—pinch me—dreams of glory. The finals will be on ESPN. Thirteen major league scouts sit in the first row behind home plate, their Jugs speed guns and stop watches ready. For David Trexler, the Cal Ripken-sized shortstop who hits number three in the order, the dream is not entirely unrealistic. Trexler is a prospect.

As the series gets under way, the biggest and noisiest clutch of fans is the group that has come the farthest, from Carolina. Nearly a hundred strong, they wave plastic bottles filled with coins. They fill the air with rhythmic clapping and tobacco-country drawls of relief—"That's a cain a corn"—or anguish—"Yore messin' a good gime, blue." A bearded, self-appointed cheerleader orchestrates a collective "R-O-W-A-N." Among the crowd are David Trexler's parents and both sets of grandparents. His dad, who runs a trucking company in Gold Hill ("Just a wide spot in the road"), is a nervous wreck. His mom has the video camera glued to her right eye as Rowan squeaks by Midland, Michigan, two to one. David fields everything that comes his way at shortstop, but he hits the ball only to the third baseman. Three ground outs and a strikeout.

Were you a little anxious, David?

"Yes Sir, maybe I was."

Trailing Rapid City, South Dakota, two-to-nothing the next day, Trexler comes to bat with two on and two outs in the eighth. The tension matches the bleacher-stomping din from the stands as he works the count to three-and-two against a hard-throwing right-hander. "Guh-DYE, David. Guh-DYE." Trexler drives the next pitch into the right field corner for a triple that ties the game. Then he drills a single to center during Rowan's winning, tenth-inning rally, and the Carolinians break out their cellular phones to dial area code 704.

Now only four teams are alive, and the boys from Carolina are clear favorites among Roseburg fans. The "home" team, from Vancouver,

Washington, got eliminated early and—with its urban cool and reserve—won no hearts off the field. Maybe baseball loves country kids more. Maybe southerners simply have more fun. Maybe baseball loves fanatics not so much as it loves good old-fashioned manners.

"I haven't heard so many yessirs and nosirs," says a Legionnaire grilling hot dogs, "since I was in the army."

Many dreams are being played out here in Roseburg, but Rowan County's hopes for a national championship hit the rocks with two consecutive losses. Baseball is tough on dreams. David Trexler's, too, will be put on hold. The professional scouts left Roseburg early, and not one had a word with Trexler. A realist might remember that the scouts are looking not for the best teams but for the best individual talent, which may or may not reach the ALWS. If Trexler has the right stuff, he'll get another chance to show it as shortstop at North Carolina State, next spring.

The Rowan County fans, wise enough to know what the dream was, will soon forget the scores but remember the trip. They'll remember the warm reception in Roseburg, where baseball lies near the core of the culture. If the accelerated pace of life in America tends to drive a wedge between amateur baseball and city people, baseball can still remind folks from opposite sides of the continent what they have in common.

Granddad Grover Trexler is a man of few words, but at tournament's end he has something to say. He's had a good time. "Roseburg," says Grover Trexler, who has never in his life been so far away, "made us feel right at home."

—*Robin Cody*

Coming Home

A baseball cap from Rowan County, North Carolina, propped on his head, Bob Weast made light of how he and a buddy had come to drive nearly 3,000 miles just to see a bunch of high school boys play ball. "We just decided we'd drive here," Mr. Weast told a newspaper reporter from the Roseburg *News-Review* during the 1996 American Legion World Series in Roseburg.

A consummate eavesdropper, I had to smile, imagining the two men sitting behind me—both sixty-something dairy farmers—hopping into a motor home on a lark and tooling across the country. "Oregon sure is a gorgeous state," Mr. Weast said in a sweet drawl. "Awful pretty." But never did he mention wanting to stick around—no chance of mistaking him for the California tourists who vacation in the Northwest and say they never want to leave. Mr. Weast knew where he belonged.

When my father had called earlier that Sunday to alert me that the Rowan team was in Roseburg, I had waffled about whether to make the seventy-mile trip south from Eugene, along Interstate 5, to the game. American Legion baseball games had been the center of my social life on the hot humid nights of my high school summers. But it had been eleven years, more than one-third of my life, since I'd considered myself a Salisbury resident.

I had left the pre-Revolutionary War city of Salisbury, Rowan County's seat, without so much as a scant look back in 1985. Though I went just forty-some miles down the road to attend Wake Forest University in Winston-Salem, the move was much more symbolic for me. My plan was to escape the small-town politics, the claustrophobia I felt every time my views didn't line up with the status quo, the stares I noticed whenever I would arrive at a local pizza hangout with a friend of a different race, the awkwardness I felt—at nearly six feet tall, outspoken and strong minded— in a land of petite, often demure, women who were well dressed and well coifed. Salisbury's female success story, after all, was Elizabeth "Liddy" Dole. Although she's a powerful woman, it always seemed to me she was best regarded for having made it while still staying a Southern Lady. Long before becoming the belle of D.C., she'd been homecoming queen both at Boyden High School (now Salisbury High) and Duke University.

I couldn't play that part. And, as a result, never quite felt like I fit in, despite winning high school honors, editing the school newspaper and yearbook, or keeping stats for three years for the Salisbury High baseball team.

I thought the problem was the place. That things were different elsewhere. That most places weren't as racist or small-minded as the small-town South. And I simply had to go find them. After college, I went looking, taking newspaper jobs in Indianapolis, Rochester (New York) and Eugene, the last, of course, considered among the most open-minded cities in America.

But soon after I arrived in Eugene in 1990, I had a state police trooper tell me he didn't think Hitler was all wrong about blacks. I learned Oregon had its own dubious history of Ku Klux Klan activity. I watched the emergence of an anti-homosexual campaign that played on fears far more than on reality. And I found left-wing liberals who were as self-righteous and closed-minded as the conservative good ol' boys from the South.

Sitting in the stands at the American Legion World Series, I couldn't help thinking about all that.

It was only after my father told me that Jim DeHart, who'd coached Salisbury High baseball when I kept stats for the team, was the coach for the Rowan Legion team that I decided to go to Roseburg. I pulled my old Salisbury High Hornets baseball cap—the one I wore two years ago when I painted my living room—out of the closet, thinking it would help trigger Coach DeHart's memory. I needn't have. As soon as I mounted the stands in Roseburg, his wife said hello. Even Steve Phillips, the *Salisbury Post* sportswriter, recognized me from my days in the Salisbury High dugout.

"You probably know my father," I said to Mr. Weast as the second inning came to a close. "I'm Joni James, Dr. James's daughter."

He slapped his knee and threw me a big smile. "I sure do. Used to work on my cows. I just saw him the other day, driving through a stoplight in his truck."

"I hope the light was green," I joked.

Mr. Weast smiled. "Oh, sure thing, honey." By the seventh-inning stretch, Mr. Weast had taken it upon himself to introduce me to most of the folks around us, fellow Rowan County fans who'd made the 3,000-mile trip to see a bunch of teenage boys play for their first national title. I'd learned which of the county's five high schools most of the players attended, and I'd joined in shouting their first names as they stepped into the batter's box. I even met Mr. and Mrs. Trexler, parents of the team's star, David, who everyone was proud of because he'd won a baseball scholarship to North Carolina State University.

I already knew some of the almost 100 fans from Rowan, recognizing them from those steamy summer nights at the Legion ball field when Mr. Bradley's hot dogs were my steady diet. Back then, the Legion games were the premier hang-out for Rowan County teens—a welcome relief from the Pudgie's Pizza-by-the-slice and Putt-Putt golf course and video arcade we relied on during the school year. Each Legion season, I'd cycle through a collection of crushes on players and fellow teenage fans, feeling safe practicing my flirting in a well-lit ball park; hoping to impress some boy that I knew a double play was marked 6-4-3 in the book; believing I was part of the win when cheers left me with a raspy postgame voice.

More than a decade later on a cool Oregon evening, the Rowan fans still believed they were part of the team, still believed rowdy behavior could turn a game. When not yelling, "C'mon now" or "You can do it," they were rattling the other team's pitcher by shaking plastic bottles filled with coins. It wasn't, however, enough. Playing a team from Yardley, Pennsylvania, the Rowan boys handed them an eight-to-seven win, committing too many errors and leaving thirteen players on base—including three in the ninth inning. One of only four teams left in the tournament, Rowan would get another chance in the double-elimination series. Unfortunately, the boys would lose that game too.

But when the Rowan players walked off the field that Sunday night, heads hanging, the fans still stood outside the gate, patting the boys on the back as they walked by, reminding them how far they'd come. I stood there with them. No one thought much of it. It was where I belonged.

—*Joni James*

Guy Maynard is the editor of *Oregon Quarterly*.

Robert Leo Heilman is a writer who lives in Myrtle Creek, Oregon, and a former catcher. A longer version of this essay appeared in *The Home Field: Nine Innings of Baseball Writing* from Sasquatch Books in Seattle. Heilman is a Contract Advisor for the Oregon Local of the National Writers Union.

Robin Cody is a Portland writer and a former shortstop and umpire. He is the author of a novel, *Ricochet River,* and *Voyage of the Summer Sun*, a nonfiction account of the author's solo canoe trip down the Columbia River.

Joni James was a reporter for *The Register-Guard* in Eugene when she wrote this piece. She is now with the *Miami Herald* in Tallahassee, Florida, a little closer to Rowan County, North Carolina.

This piece appeared in the Spring 1997 issue of *Oregon Quarterly.*

When He Falls Off a Horse

Debra Gwartney

An accident brings together father and daughter, past and present, toughness and vulnerability.

The dead of night phone call that woke me was from Becky, my youngest sister. She wasn't calling from her home in Seattle, but from the Boise hospital, where she'd arrived after a late flight. Her news was about our dad. About a rodeo accident. I stood in the dark of my Tucson house, my family asleep, as Becky told me what had happened earlier in the day. Dad had been flagging for a cutting competition when a brawl of activity got his horse, Sweet, riled. Sweet bucked in a tight corner while Dad leaned in to try to regain control. The horse suddenly lurched and slammed the back of his head into my father's face, knocking him unconscious. Dad fell backward with reins looped around his wrist, landing in powdery sawdust butt up, yanking 1,200-pound Sweet on top of him. Two men who drove my father's wife behind the ambulance described the horse landing with a sprawled thud: the jerked-short cries of man and animal then the splintered noise of thin ice giving way under heavy boots; eerie, groaning cracks as bone split and tissue burst.

My sister had arrived minutes before the surgeon emerged from the back of the hospital, after a nine-hour operation, to tell my father's wife that a lung had been crushed, a kidney destroyed, the spleen shredded. The spinal cord itself was intact—a miracle—but he said surgeons couldn't cobble together enough bone from smashed vertebrae to reencase the cord. They'd never seen such a pebbled mess. "They told the doctors that when they pulled the horse off, Dad was folded in half going the wrong way," Becky said.

My father was sixteen when I was born, a sophomore in high school. I'm the product of a backseat date between the Salmon High basketball team captain and his cheerleader girlfriend. Such an ordinary small town story, but true: my maternal grandparents offering to pitch in for college if he promised to never contact my mother; those same grandparents slipping adoption counselors into their home to persuade my mother to preserve her future. And my father's parents—what I heard from my aunt when she decided I was old enough to know about my beginning was that news of the pregnancy prompted the one crying episode of my grandfather's life. He wept in his leather recliner in the corner of the den, bent like an old nail.

No matter his father's tears, my father would do what he wanted, what he thought best. What he wanted was to prove he could make it against any odds. He married my seventeen-year-old mother, who accepted a domestic life in a travel trailer set on a dusty patch between my father's family home and the county jail. The two walked around the corner to the justice of the peace to wed after school let out that summer, 1957. I was born three weeks later, weighing a few ounces over four pounds. The way my father describes it—when he's in the mood to recount his youth—his job was to flick my feet with the edge of a fingernail so I'd stay awake long enough to drink an ounce of milk.

I don't remember that, of course. Nor do I have distinct memories of my father through my childhood—just flashes. After I was born, I understand, he gave up basketball and cowboying to finish high school (an old film shows year-younger Cindy and me watching my parents' graduation from the bleachers) and get to college. When they settled into the small university town, two more babies popped out like corn on a stalk, cramming our trailer with fat diapers, moist beds, squeaky toys and hand-me-down clothes steeped in stranger stench. My father got up early to deliver milk, bringing home cartons of leftover cottage cheese, expired half-and-half, ice cream, before heading to class. At night and on weekends he worked at the gas station two blocks from the trailer court. Saturdays, Mom bundled her four children in our wagon and pulled us down to where he filled tanks and cleaned bugs off windows, taking him soup and bread, a red apple. Before we left, he'd sometimes sweep down and gather up my sister and me, one under each arm. He'd set me on one side of the lift used to get cars off the ground and Cindy on the other, instructing us to hang on. Then he'd pull the lever to raise us a few feet from the floor, a sort of greasy carnival ride. My eyes stung from the sticky cloud of lubricants in the garage as we rumbled off the ground, but I tightened my grip around the metal bar and steadied a flinchless watch on Cindy, and she on me.

By the time I was six, we'd moved to Boise so he could work for a large timber company. I was old enough, by then, to wonder how he fit with the rest of the family. His work kept him on the road most weeks, and often when he reappeared I'd have to remind myself that he was not a stranger. One night during my first-grade year he came home from his first big trip, a journey to New York. He slumped through the door under a dark coat, complaining about his long day, about crazy airports and clogged freeways, as he set his briefcase on the edge of the couch and sprung its latches. Nearby, my mother, with Becky attached to her leg, wound her hands in a kitchen towel, nodding as he talked. Cindy, Ron, and I sat on the living room floor under the lamp light, building with Lincoln Logs, weaving a green fence around our simple cabin. Dad pulled a folded rectangle out of the interior pocket of the case and, with a whip of his wrist, waved it open. Red silk sailed over our heads, the blue and

Debra Gwartney

green Statue of Liberty in the center trembling in the light. My mother grinned and murmured appreciation with her tired voice, the one that sent us slipping to our rooms when we heard it in the evenings. I turned to look fully at the gift-bearer. I knew he was Dad, half the mom-and-dad pair of every family, but I couldn't quite make sense of how that worked. I couldn't all the way explain to myself what he had to do with me.

When he was home, we knew to stay quiet and out of his way. No races to the barometer hanging at the end of the hall, no jumping on the bed to Nancy Sinatra's boot song. When he was home, the television showed Saturday and Sunday afternoon ball games, not cartoons, not Lassie. My mother set up a TV tray in front of him on those days. She brought him a tuna sandwich and a pile of chips arranged on a plate, a sweaty glass of Coke. While he ate, the three of us, and later Becky, slipped down the narrow passage from our bedroom to squeeze between sofa and wall. We had to wait only minutes folded in back of the couch before he'd suddenly launch from his seat, a rocket, to scream and stomp at the players on the screen, chips flying like confetti and soda splashing across the floor. "Stupid! Idiots!" he'd yell, while we shoved our faces into the thin carpet or the scratchy sofa upholstery to muffle our laughter. "Learn to play the goddamned game!"

When we were older Dad sometimes took the four of us to his weekly basketball practice for the intramural team he played on, bringing us along to give my mother an evening's respite from a houseful of children. One bitterly cold night we'd gone to a junior high gym, over-warm and ripe with smells from the glistening bustle of men on the floor, their shoes squeaking across the smooth surface as they jostled each other under the basket. Cindy, Ron and I climbed up and down the bleachers, rattling the planks and metal braces, slipping underneath to seek still-wrapped gum or sticky coins, while peeling off layers of our clothes. Becky, who was seven, ran after us, pleading for us to include her.

When it was time to leave, we reluctantly re-dressed, bundling in coats and hats—still sweaty hot even standing in the draft at the big doors leading to the parking lot. As soon as my dad swung open the door, though, the first blast of cold air propelled us toward the car. "Take your hands out of your pockets," he said as we dashed across the frozen asphalt.

Three of us instantly yanked our bare hands free of that inner warmth, but Becky didn't, keeping her small fingers shoved deep in the interior of her parka as she scurried to keep up. Within two or three steps, she hit a patch of ice and, like a slippery seal, flipped into the air, crashing face first into the pavement. Cindy and I turned and ran back toward the light of the gym door and our squalling sister, Cindy reaching her first, pulling now-screaming Becky to her feet. Blood gushed from her mouth and nose and seeped across her bright pink hands, which flung wildly at her wounds. By that time, our father had caught up with the scene. He strode past without breaking his rhythm, heading to the car without hesitation.

"Better learn to listen," he said.

That was his way. A no-nonsense way. Sometimes I was afraid of him; often I considered him mean. What I couldn't recognize then was that this matter-of-fact exterior was the way he was going to make sure he made it. Back then, I couldn't see the rare determination and ambition with which my father supported his family. He not only finished college, but did a stint of graduate studies at Harvard while my mother stayed home with us. He became vice president of one of the largest companies in the Northwest. He got wealthy. He and my mother divorced after twenty-five years and he married a socialite widow, then later became involved with the younger woman who'd become his third wife.

It was when he was forty-eight and we were all gone from home that my father joined his closest friend in buying a ranch outside Boise and turning it into a rodeo grounds. *Where had this come from?* my siblings and I asked each other. *Who knew he even liked rodeo?* Events were held there each Saturday and Sunday, the place soon full on weekends with horses and cattle and people and picnic baskets.

After a thirty-two-year break, my father was a cowboy again.

I flew to Boise on a Wednesday, two mornings after receiving news of the accident. I'd put graduate school on temporary hold and arranged for my daughters' care during their father's work hours. My dad was alive and had made progress breathing on his own, but no one could promise a recovery. On the airplane, I shoved aside the scene of my departure, the two youngest girls—the baby only eighteen months—screaming for me from their father's arms, and his scowling insistence that, forget it, they'd be fine. My husband and I both knew he'd turn the children over to his mother as soon as he could. I felt an itchy burn over his eagerness to bail. I also nervously wondered what waited for me in Boise. My father's wife had told me not to come, not to disrupt my own life when there was nothing I could do to help. But I had insisted.

Cindy met me at the airport and filled me in on the latest details. Dad's wife, whose son had died of leukemia in the same hospital, couldn't bring herself to come in much after the first wave of crisis, so my sisters had agreed to stay through both days and nights. Someone had to be there at all times to ensure he got the right attention: his cracked lips moistened, his bluish feet kept propped on pillows. Once an hour, Becky and Cindy gingerly took hold of either side of the thick sheepskin placed under him and scooted it minutely, one inch, to ease the pressure on his skin. Other than that, he was not to move. A sign above his head warned against accidentally nudging him, as his spinal cord was completely unsheathed.

Cindy described how things were going, sighed, then glanced back at her two young children buckled in the backseat of her car.

"You stay home tonight, I'll take over," I said.

Cindy nodded. "I'm so tired." Pausing, she looked over at me. "I'm pregnant again."

"Oh," I said, not sure of the response she wanted.

"We're happy, we're glad, another baby will be wonderful," she rushed to say. "But I know Dad will be mad. He wants us to get stable. He'll say we're not ready."

I reached over to grab her hand.

"It's great news," I said, squeezing her fingers.

"Don't tell him, okay?" she said.

Of course I wouldn't. Besides, I had my own trouble to confess. The erosion of my marriage, like a house encroached by a landslide. The move to Arizona, graduate school—things I'd told my dad would keep us together that had added to the crumbling, had pushed the house down the hill. I'd stopped hoping for what would save us and lately had begun to seek a little grace for the children as the marriage came whirling apart. But how could I tell my father?

I stood at the door of his ICU room thinking that he looked like an overstuffed turkey ready for the oven. His purple body was bloated to nearly double its size. Tubes ran from his mouth, chest, belly, groin, each carrying a different color of liquid—green, yellow, white—collecting in bottles under the bed. One side of his face was beaten to the color and texture of hamburger. A machine huffed, released, pushing air into his one working lung, filling the room with its rhythm. The IV beeped in time.

He didn't know I was there; he stayed slipped away at first. I went to work with my sisters. Though we were warned not to touch the morphine button—only the patient is to administer, the nurses scolded—we punched it every eight minutes. If we forgot, Dad moaned from some deep place. Every hour, we moved him an inch, causing more pinched groaning and a pained grimace. Now and then I glimpsed the ragged stitches that made him look like he was laced from the base of the neck to his tailbone.

Doctors decided to remove the respirator Friday morning. Once taking his own shallow breaths, Dad began to orient to the room—he looked around, one eye peeping under its fat purple pocket, taking in the complicated morass of equipment over his head and around him. He muttered one of our names if he wanted water or another blanket. By Saturday, he actually spoke a bit—sometimes making sense, though now and then he'd ask us to unstrap him from the barber's chair. He'd beg us to untie invisible ropes from around his legs.

Sunday, as early morning light streamed through the windows, three doctors came in to say that a surgeon in Baltimore had agreed to rebuild my father's spinal column with metal. Once he was stable, he and his wife would fly there for the operation.

"I guess you folks know how amazing it is that the cord is intact," one doctor said. "Just one little nick is all. It's unbelievable he survived." He stepped to the bedside to look down at my dad. "You're going to be the star of my next convention, I'll tell you that. I can't wait to show your X-rays."

"You'd better make goddamn sure I get all the credit," my dad said. I called my husband to say I was coming home.

My last night, around midnight, Dad woke up and asked for television. "See if there's a movie," he said, tipping his head forward—his only allowed movement besides moving his arms. I picked up the remote and eventually found an old John Wayne film. I scooted a chair over to watch with him. It was as awake as he'd been and the first time he'd addressed me like he knew who I was. Staring up at the ceiling, he asked about my children, about graduate school. He nodded over at Cindy, asleep on a cot across the room. "You know, she's pregnant again," he said. I said I did, and waited. He didn't go on.

Then he commented on how his wife had not been up to see him much. Again, I nodded.

"The thing about marriage," he said then, out of nowhere, "is that the only people who know what's going on are the ones behind the closed door at night."

I don't know where that sentence came from. I don't know if he was referring to his marriage or mine, but it was what allowed me to call a year later—two months after he'd cut off his full-body cast and thrown it in the back field and a month after he was back on Sweet, riding in the evenings along the riverbank—to tell him I was leaving my husband. Without a complaint, he offered help and sent me a check for an attorney and rent for a townhouse.

But this night in the hospital I sat in the dark room silently, wondering how to begin to say all I wanted to.

"You know what I feel like?" he said then, stretching his arms above his head. "A cup of hot chocolate."

"I'll find some for you." I jumped to my feet, dashing to the nurses station, where I learned that a vending machine was my only hope. I began combing the halls of each floor until I found—on the seventh— the correct machine. I put in quarters and watched steaming liquid fill the cup. When I returned to my dad's room, he was asleep again, down deep, lulled by the soft beeps of the equipment and John Wayne's husky voice. I considered waking him, but realized there was nothing else to talk about. I put the chocolate on the table beside him, hoping that even if he didn't taste it, he'd notice it there. I tucked the blankets over his shoulders and made sure his feet were on the pillow.

Then I sat back down in my chair to watch him sleep.

Debra Gwartney is a Eugene, Oregon, freelance writer and teacher. She has published memoir in such journals and magazines as *Creative Nonfiction, Fourth Genre, Salon* and *Open Spaces.*

This essay was the winner of the 2000 *Oregon Quarterly* Northwest Perspectives Essay Contest. It appeared in the Summer 2000 issue of *Oregon Quarterly.*

Army Men

Paul Keller

Sometimes the heroes are closer to home than you think.

My father walks into the room.

Along with every other boy in my neighborhood, I love war. *Combat*
—a fictional World War II infantry saga—is my favorite TV show. Whenever I hear or whistle the theme song, I feel good about myself. All brave
and strong and patriotic.

My dad—who never watches television—stops.

He stands there looking down at the screen. I start hoping he might sit
and see how good my favorite show is. That he might get to know these
cool World War II army guys just as well as I do.

"That's nuts. They'd never move through an open area like that."

He says it matter-of-factly and shakes his head like this is all kind of
silly and just a bit foolish and pretend. He smiles at me. Then he walks on
down the hall into his downstairs office.

My dad was an infantry foot soldier in World War II. But that was easy to forget. This genial guy who wore wing tips and ties and didn't hunt or fish or swear or smoke or swig booze—didn't really match my generation's John Wayne-warrior stereotype. And, like so many other fathers, my dad never really talked about those war years.

As I grew up, I only heard a few of his army stories. Usually the ones that made you laugh.

How when they first got off the ship in the Philippines, this guy pretended to stumble and pitched his rifle into the ocean—in hopes he wouldn't have to go into the jungles to fight. Or the guy from the South who always swore to God that if he ever made it back home, he was gonna leave his goddamn rifle (that he'd had to clean every day since boot camp) out in his barn and go piss on it every morning for the rest of his life. My dad would tell that story, endearingly repeat the guy's name to himself a few times, and chuckle.

But, when I got older, my mom told me how both of these men—and so many others who served alongside my dad—came home in swollen blue-black pieces inside military caskets.

It was after high school, with Vietnam exploding into our headlines, that my mom told me more about my dad and that war. Like when his company's captain went berserk from fear, how my dad was promoted in the field. At that time, they were losing many, many people in bloody fighting trying to claim a strategic mountain pass.

During this campaign, a teenage private approached my dad one morning and told him he had a terrible stomachache and couldn't go back out into combat. He begged my dad to send him to the rear. He even broke down and cried. My dad, nonetheless, told him no. He convinced him that he would be okay, that he needed to go fight.

The kid was killed that day.

Afterwards, my dad radioed headquarters and refused to send another person up there until the enemy positions had been heavily shelled. He was told that wasn't possible and threatened with a court-martial. My dad—a man who would never bend or break a rule—still refused. The powers that be finally conceded. He was never court-martialed.

My mom started to cry when she told me, "I know your father still thinks about that boy. He was probably about your age."

Last spring I contacted a few people who had known my dad before I was born. I wanted to understand more about this man who was suddenly taken from us by cancer at age sixty-seven.

A man who had served with him in World War II wrote back from the other side of the country: "Your father was one of the bravest men I ever knew. When we were pinned down in the Sierra Madre Mountains east of Manila, I can still see him jump up in the face of heavy enemy fire and rally our company forward. He wasn't reckless or foolish, he just did what needed to be done."

As my forty-nine-year-old eyes read those words, they filled with tears. I had so many questions for my father. I will always regret that I never asked them.

In the last scene on *Combat* after the final commercial that night in 1962 when my dad had come through the TV room, Kirby and Cage cradled their Hollywood rifles, eyed the camera and spoke their macho lines to me and so many other American grade-schoolers. But before their beloved theme song even started, I stood and snapped the set off.

I kept thinking about what my dad had said.

Paul Keller is a writer and editor for the U.S. Forest Service's national office. His poetry has appeared in *Wilderness, Appalachia, Chicago Review* and other publications. He lives near Mt. Hood in the Oregon Cascades.

This essay appeared in the Summer 2000 issue of *Oregon Quarterly.*

Finding Frogs

Cheri Brooks

Love, territory and amphibians.

In January, red-legged frogs make love in breeding ponds. During the summer they live by running streams or in the moist underbrush under sword ferns. Sometime after Halloween they move back toward the ponds. But they disappear for a while. Where do they spend Thanksgiving? Where do they spend Christmas? That's what Chris wants to find out.

It's 6:00 A.M. and we pull up next to a green mini-van in the IHOP parking lot off Interstate 5. Marc Hayes is waiting inside, along with his wife, Charleen, and a biology student named Rombough, who is wearing shorts on this foggy November morning. They have awakened in the middle of the night to travel a hundred miles south from Portland. Hayes is a biologist like Chris. Charleen, Rombough and I are just along for the ride. We'll drive for three more hours into the mountains and then we will look for frogs.

I rarely go into the field with Chris. I'm usually too busy working at my office job or spending time with my daughter. When I have the chance, I join the throngs of other urbanites on the jogging trail or soccer field or at the dog park. Though Chris and I have dated for several years, we live separate lives, seeing each other mostly at night or during the weekends. He knows how to navigate a forest but has some trouble finding his way inside my small family. This Sunday, I'm tagging along to find out where he disappears to in the spring. I want to learn about the amphibial attractions of wet bogs and brush thickets and high, cold mountain lakes.

Driving south toward the Umpqua Basin, Chris and Hayes discuss ecological meetings, writing grants and which journals are best to publish in; scientist talk. They weigh the possibilities of sacrificing a couple of female red-legged frogs, slitting them open and counting their eggs. Hayes tells Chris about articles he's published and terrain where he found lots of amphibians. They laugh about a group from the Portland Zoo, brought out by Hayes a couple of weeks earlier. One woman held up a sprig of poison oak and asked him, "What is *this* pretty plant?"

Chris is just beginning his herpetology career, even though he's always caught slimy things. He was the kind of kid who turned over logs to look for salamanders, who kept frogs in his pockets. I keep a copy of a photo that shows him as a freckled nine-year-old staring eye-to-eye with a rat snake. Now he's learning about the territorial behavior of biologists.

It's something he talks about at the end of a long day, in frustrated tones. Researchers must divide up Oregon's frogs and toads and snakes and salamanders, competing for funding and study sites. But Chris and Hayes have decided to follow the red-legged frogs of Squaw Flat together.

By the time we get to Canyonville, the sun is rising over the Cascades. The hills are inky against the blank-page sky. As we climb higher the pavement turns to gravel and then to dirt. Hayes noses the van against a berm. We notice a deep puddle in the ditch, where dirt has been scooped out to end the road. Next to the muddy hole, a large red-legged frog sits serenely.

They can tell she's female because female frogs are bigger than males. Males have bulkier biceps and larger thumbs with "nuptial pads," which they use for grasping their partners during mating. This girl has long flipper feet fringed in red, which stretch out surprisingly far when Hayes grasps her around the middle. When he clips a scale to her ankle and hangs her upside down, she dangles gracefully like a gymnast on the uneven bars, one leg bent. She weighs seventy-five grams and measures ninety-six millimeters.

Hayes waves a telephone-sized scanner across her back, but gets no response. He uses a nail clipper to open a small slit in her mossy skin. She doesn't flinch. He rubs a rice-grain-sized chip into the opening, rolling it upward into the nape of her neck. Then he scans the frog again, and she beeps back at him and registers a display of digits. A moment later she once again is sitting next to her puddle, camouflaging into the mud.

"It's going to be a good day," Chris says.

Everyone begins unloading the gear from the van and putting on rubber boots. Rombough changes into army fatigues. He tells Hayes that he wants to find out if the camo garb will help him capture more frogs compared with, say, a white T-shirt. He is a freshman in college, a kind of biological prodigy whom Hayes has mentored for several years. On a good day, Chris tells me, Rombough out-catches everybody.

As we head down the trail toward the prairie, Rombough scampers around turning over rocks, disemboweling rotting logs, and scraping through bark. He finds a bright-green tree frog, a little guy with raccoon eyes. He is weighed and measured and let go. Only six grams, too small for cataloging.

Rombough disappears for a while as we approach the prairie, and Hayes keeps turning around to look for him. Suddenly, Rombough emerges with a tiny clouded salamander. Its toes are square, made for climbing trees. Everyone admires the find, and Rombough tells me that these creatures live between layers of bark, eating ants.

We walk through the lush moss layer of an open Douglas-fir forest. Chris hikes stiff-legged in his tall rubber boots, using his net handle to poke and prod the turf. I can see the peak of his cap bobbing over branches. Chris walks gently in the woods, though he's a big man. When we arrive at the prairie, Hayes crouches a bit and rustles carefully through the grass like someone looking for lost keys. I think: They are trying to imagine themselves in the hidden world of the dead and decaying, a pungent realm inches from the ground.

The prairie is shrinking, Hayes tells me. Because the Forest Service has not let the area burn, conifers are encroaching onto the open savanna. Egg-laying reptiles, like pond turtles and snakes, nest in the prairies where the ground is warm enough to incubate their eggs. He says the plateau has more reptile and amphibian diversity than any place on Oregon's westside. It contains species that live both at low and high elevations from across the Northwest. And it's relatively undisturbed. For him it's the perfect place to figure out where red-legged frogs go during the winter when they leave the forest streams to breed.

We sweep the prairie but find no frogs. At the edge of the plateau we decide to split up. Hayes, Charleen and Rombough will search a draw running toward the big creek below. Chris and I will head downstream along a narrow seep.

Ours is a more gradual descent. It's nice to be alone with Chris in a part of the world where he feels so comfortable. His nets and notebooks and forest-green wardrobe make sense out here. Such things are out of place in my home. I don't like it when I find dead bullfrogs in my freezer, or when his wet boots smell so rank that I have to put them outside. I do not keep piles of rubber and plastic and polypropylene in my living room, as Chris does. My daughter and I don't sip canned soup directly from the pot. We don't heap journals and stacks of papers across our bedrooms, clearing only a shallow path from desk to door.

Most of my friends are married. Their husbands watch football, play golf, mow the lawn, work nine to five, wear a tie to work. Chris says he owns three ties, but I've never seen him wear one. He dislikes football and thinks golf is boring. He shuns domestic chores. He makes awkward conversation with my daughter and can't understand her teenage desires. They are like ships running aground on each other's terrain.

The ground along the seep is rutted by deep pools covered with grass. I walk and wonder where I might go if I were a frog. And I know the place when I see it—a small pool framed by fallen logs. Sure enough, I spot a Cascade frog posing as a piece of fallen bark. Cascade frogs are closely related to red-leggeds, but their undersides are creamy with a yellow-green tinge. I proudly catch my first amphibian, who has knobby thumbs and bulging biceps. Chris takes him from me and puts him through the routine of weighing, measuring, scanning, clipping, inserting the chip. "Good boy," he tells the frog.

Downstream in the next pool, we find a male red-legged. Chris holds him toward me and tells me to sniff. The frog's moist skin gives off a slightly bitter odor, something like parsley. Chris explains it's a chemical compound that makes the frog unpalatable to predators. This prey fights and kicks as he hangs from the scale. He jerks when his skin is clipped. Chris says, "It's all right, big guy."

In another pool we see a great, Cleopatra-like female with gold-shadowed eyelids. Her flippers are rose-colored, the shade of Indian paintbrush. Chris admires her beauty and photographs her on the sunny bank. He calls her "sweetie," something he has never called me.

Chris has nicknames for me but none that are very flattering. He calls me "grump" or "doofus," and he likes to make fun of my long spidery fingers and lack of grace. When I complain, he tells me it's how he shows his affection. On Valentine's Day, he gave me a photo of an Oregon spotted frog with these words scrawled on the back: "Happy V-Day Doofus. Love, Frogs 'R' Us!" Sometimes, he leans over as if to kiss me, but instead he blows into the side of my cheek as if pushing away the tender moment. In the woods among frogs, though, our awkwardness melts into the filtered afternoon light.

The more we walk along the seep, the more frogs we find. They practically jump into our laps. I mostly stay out of the way and record the data, but sometimes I stroke their sticky skin. We've caught eleven frogs when it's time to meet Hayes again. The seep is a frog highway. Are they always here? I hardly ever see such things when I'm not with Chris. Maybe he knows where to look. Or maybe he knows how to speak to them.

We meet the others at the van. Rombough is eating lunch out of a big cooler that his mother packed. He, Hayes and Charleen found only a couple of frogs in the deep draw. When we tell them we caught eleven, their eyes grow wide.

Our next stop is a stagnant pool covered with duckweed, where Hayes thinks red-leggeds might be congregating. Chris and Rombough head uphill, backtracking in terrain they covered on a previous trip. There's some confusion about the number of prairies surrounding the breeding area. The landscape does not match Hayes's aerial photos.

At the duckweed pond, Hayes finds plenty of red-leggeds, Cascades and hybrids between the two. He sneaks up on each one, snatching his quarry like a frog himself. He catches dozens—nearly every frog he sees —but that is not enough. He wants to capture and weigh and scan and clip and tag every amphibian in the pond. All the captures get stored in zip-lock bags until its time to go, so he doesn't catch the same one twice.

When Rombough and Chris return, they're disappointed. They didn't find anything except the frogs Chris and I caught earlier. They're tired and irritable. Chris is ready to leave. It's been a long day, and there are still several hours of driving ahead. But we've learned something about where the frogs go during winter. Hayes guesses they'll hide in the murky duckweed pond until it's time to breed.

We ride home in darkness. Hayes manages to remain alert after six hours of driving and eight hours of frogging. He and Chris talk some more about upcoming conferences and a paper they're writing together. They tell each other frog stories, like the time Hayes saw a marsh hawk drop a large garter snake it was carrying. Hayes recovered the dead snake and realized that its stomach was quite full. So he carved it open and found an unblemished spotted frog inside. Later, he opened the spotted frog's stomach and discovered baby toads. I guess when you look for frogs, you sometimes find the unexpected.

Chris and Hayes are going to write a paper about *bufivory*, a term that Chris coined after noticing spotted frogs in a high Cascade lake eating juveniles of the toad species *Bufo boreas*. Sometimes I call Chris "Bufo borealis" because he's grouchy and solitary and nocturnal like a toad. He's distant in the van, putting a cold river between us in the back seat. And I am anxious to get home to my daughter. We will go back to our separate lives. He will stay up late reading e-mails. I will cook a hot dinner, get ready for work and go to bed. I've had enough of Chris for one day.

But I have a fondness for amphibians. Last year when I traveled to Brazil to visit my sister, a palm-sized tree frog leaped from the ceiling of our hotel room and landed on my shoulder. I considered it quite an honor —to be chosen by a Brazilian frog. I would rather kiss a frog than a prince. Perhaps that is why I love Chris. I like the way his eyes change from green to brown and back again and how he navigates around a mountain or reaches into the mud and finds a croaking matriarch. I know that tomorrow or maybe the next day, I'll hear his unvoiced plea. And we'll be drawn back into each other's circles for a spell.

Cheri Brooks lives in Eugene, Oregon. Her work has appeared in various local and regional publications, as well as two anthologies, *The Book of the Tongass* and *Reflections on a Life with Diabetes*.

This essay was the second-place winner in the 2000 *Oregon Quarterly* Northwest Perspectives Essay Contest.

Waiting Out the Wind

Mark Blaine

One writer watches his footprints in the changing sands of the Oregon Dunes.

At the Oregon Dunes, the sea makes its smoothest transition to the hard land of the Oregon Coast. The sand is nearly liquid in its movement, and the windward landscape appears in soft focus: Where the ground begins and the air ends is indefinite. The grains shift by bouncing against each other like tiny billiard balls. Most grains carried by the wind sail only a few feet before they land and bounce off others, launching those into the relentless blow. While strong winds can carry them great distances, they are, after all, little stones, crushed Cascade Mountains carried to the ocean by the Umpqua River, and they have a finite trajectory. The hard physics of ballistics may best describe their movement. They're bullets with a talent for finding mucous membranes. Eyes blink and water, teeth feel an extra crunch.

The top three inches of moving sand will scour bare skin raw in minutes, and most animals, purposeful ones who don't hike for sport, just pass through the open dunes on their way to better food, warmer shelter, and others of their kind. Errant seeds gain little purchase.

At the bottom of the biggest dune, I am protected. In its lee, air eddies in a confused swirl that seems still compared to the blasts of wind coursing across the dunes from the Pacific Ocean. Near the trail markers, thousands of footprints indicate the path to the beach. I have come to see this landscape, to get a sense of its contour, and a well-beaten hollow between dunes is just one feature. Off trail, wandering the sands, I might get away from people, away from their effects. So I climb.

At the ridgetop, my view is better. I can see ocean to the west and dense forest and clearcuts of the Coast Range to the east. Following the ridgeline, it's easy walking on the gentle slope of the crest and I continue without, I feel, much aim. My eyes seek perspective, shifting between distance and detail. My breathing eases and my heart slows, following the contour I walk. The loose fabric of my T-shirt flaps. The skin of my forearms grows rubbery and chill in the salt air, the wind carrying my body heat away. The sand works into my shoes and I feel grit between my toes. I reach a patch of harder sand, consolidated and wet, exposed by the wind, and I stop. Here, at least, I won't be ankle deep in sand.

I turn, and when I see my footprints on the ridge blowing away, I ask myself how long they will last. I decide to wait out the wind.

We are like the aggressive weeds and exotic animals that follow us, says natural history writer David Quammen. A verdant blanket of kudzu crawls about the South, zebra mussels infest the water systems of the Great Lakes, American chestnut blight has wiped out the dominant tree of eastern forests and brown tree snakes have eaten most of the birds in Guam. In hindsight, we ask, "What kind of fool would think to bring that here and mar paradise?"

Our kind of fool, it seems. What we miss in all these darkly comic stories of invading plants and animals is the human weed. Many of the stories are rooted in simple human obliviousness: Tankers release their bilge water thousands of miles from where they collected it; snakes hitch rides on World War II bombers and hop islands across the South Pacific; somebody wants a new way to feed a cow; somebody else wants to keep the sand from blowing around.

I came to the dunes to see European beach grass, a non-native nuisance plant that, by many accounts, has devastated the Oregon Dunes National Recreation Area. Every day the grass creeps farther into the open sand of the dunes, and Ed Becker, the U.S. Forest Service ranger based in Reedsport, says they'll be grassed over in a hundred years. "It's the Oregon *Dunes*," he says, stretching the *u* in dunes for emphasis, reminding me that preserving the most important part of the name of this forty-mile-long strip of sand between Florence and Coos Bay is part of his job.

The dunes have been open sand for 6,000 years, a geologic anomaly among the rocky headlands of the Oregon Coast. A hundred years ago, local people avoided the place. They lived on its fringes, running logs down the Siuslaw, Umpqua and Coos Rivers to the ports at their mouths. But the shifting sands played havoc with river channels and blew over the roads. So seventy-five years ago, the locals, with some federal money, planted European beach grass to stabilize their public works. Neat, even rows of beach grass plantations were a pattern of progress that would defeat wind-borne randomness. So the plan went.

The Oregon Coast, however, is headstrong, a difficult beauty. Winter winds regularly blow eighty or ninety miles per hour. Waves crest at twenty feet or more and fall upon themselves with a concussive bass that thumps the sternum and robs you of breath. It's hard to find an intact shell on the beach because the breakers pulverize them before they're swept ashore. Storms get a running start from thousands of miles out in the North Pacific and then pile into the Coast Range.

Amid this violence, the grass held, but not without alteration. The coast cuts the cloth of progress to fit. Storms broke chunks of beach grass from their plantations, and currents carried the shoots to new, unintended parts of the dunes. The grass took hold, spread its runners and flourished. Progress conceded some to randomness.

Twenty-five years ago, attitudes turned, and emptiness suddenly had natural value. Congress declared the dunes a National Recreation Area, a place of unique desolation that needed to be protected from encroachment by human development.

It was too late. The grass continued its creep, defying human efforts to stop it.

European beach grass adapted to the strong winds of its native habitat off the North Atlantic by growing in thick, needle-sharp tufts. The thin stiff blades of the grass stand straight in the wind and block the grains of sand tumbling and bouncing along the surface of the dunes. The sand quickly piles up around the beach grass and buries it for a time before the grass blades grow to the surface, seeking sunlight. In this way, European beach grass appears to sink its roots up to twenty-five feet into loose sand, but it's really growing up, more like a tree, and using the sand for support. Because of this, a ridge rises just beyond the high-tide line all along the forty-mile face of the Oregon Dunes. Fifty years ago, when the mass plantings of beach grass were just taking hold, this so-called foredune didn't exist. In contrast, American dune grass, native to the Oregon Dunes, has wide floppy blades that lie flat in the wind and let the sand fly by, not pile up.

It does little to alter the landscape.

This is a place of turbulence. The clouds reflect the patterns of the dunes, running in wind-sculpted, bulging bands where the cold ocean abuts the Coast Range's foothills. Sometimes, the sun breaks free as a muted orb. Later it rains. The wind, a steady white noise, gusts but never ceases. From atop this dune, I can see inland to where the sky is clear. Or I can look out to sea, where clouds are a thin, even coat of gray, like paint on coastal houses that resists the winter wind. I'm at the center of the action, I think, but it's a false impression: The dunes amplify geology and weather.

I'm an inch short of six and a half feet, a hearty windbreak, but being warm-blooded, only good for a short stretch. The grass is more patient. It stands two- to three-feet tall above the surface of the sand, but it will grow much taller than me, its roots holding deep in the dune. The grass will completely change the way this place looks. My influence surely is more fleeting, I tell myself. I will prove it by watching my footprints blow away.

Many of my footprints fill quickly—half are gone in ten minutes. After more than thirty minutes, less than a dozen remain. I try to will them to fill. I don't feel cold, but I know I am.

I don't belong in the dunes—humans have generally stayed on their fringes—but drawn by the natural drama of doomed emptiness, I can't help but shoulder a backpack. I tell myself I can make some sense of it, but that notion is a con man.

I spent five years as a newspaper reporter learning to be a weed with a will, insinuating myself into places and relationships I would never live and could not know. For a while I wrote about a paper mill. Below it the water ran coffee brown and smelled like rotten eggs, and it seemed easy to lay blame and name fools. The people who complained loudly of the pollution were among the Appalachian poor and, presenting a convincing case (look at the water, they said), they won money for pollution damage in court. But a few were so poor that they flushed their toilets straight into the river, and the river remained polluted. The effects of poverty and malaise are harder to make into newspaper copy, and I was told my responsibilities lay elsewhere. Looking back, I can see that those words were often shabby and out of plumb, invasive. My writing pitted people against each other, against their land and against their homes. I walked away. I know those footprints remain.

Today, it's a more innocent game, and I make the rules. I won't move my feet until those old prints are gone: I must see if my presence can be erased. If someone comes upon me, my path will be a mystery. Without an obvious track, I might seem to belong more to this place. One might guess that I'd always been here.

I won't take my backpack off to put on a windbreaker. My senses need to ride this out, I tell myself, at least until they're numb from cold. Numbness, too, will be part of the experience. "Be," I tell myself in my best weekender Zen voice.

I feel odd at first just standing still, exposed on the top of the ridge, and it helps that no one is around. But evidence of people abounds. Someone named Justin has proclaimed his love for Susan by carving their names into the flat plain of sand below me. I envision him hopping backward, dragging his heel in the sand while she watches, giggling and unsure about the display, her arms wrapped around herself so she might be smaller in the wind, warmer. The letters, impermanent graffiti, are probably as tall as Justin. If all goes well, it will be a small, funny memory of their courtship. If it doesn't, those words will be lost to the wind.

But maybe not. It's nearly 4:30 on an October afternoon, and my stubborn footprints are making me wonder if I have misjudged the place, a fool caught in the headlights of his hubris. The wind isn't doing its job as quickly as I expected.

Wilbur Ternyik, a landscape consultant in Florence, once helped a man from Libya who wanted to fix a problem that the Romans created 2,000 years before. Pushing the boundaries of their empire, the Romans invaded and occupied North Africa and, in the process, denuded the natural forest, leaving rootless, shifting sands. This man wanted to fix the sands and revive the forest, and he looked up Ternyik in his Oregon coastal home for advice. Ternyik, a former mayor of Florence and a U.S. Marine wounded by a machine gun, has short gray hair bleached white around his neck and temples by the sun. His forearms are thick and his face is tan with the deep lines of a farmer. He is a rare sand stabilization expert who plants millions of European beach grass shoots, or culms, every year.

Like his Libyan client, Ternyik takes a long view of time. He's been here longer than anyone else, and he's watched the changes to the dunes.

He doesn't see much of a problem. An earthquake and tsunami hit the coast about every 300 years, and our time is nearly up, Ternyik says. A tall sand ridge, like the foredune that's grown up around European beach grass, may save coastal communities from severe damage. Locals call it a sea wall, and Ternyik doesn't think the sea wall should come down. "It would end up with a hell of a lot of people being drowned," he says.

There's irony in Ternyik's work. He's fought to preserve the open sands of the Oregon Dunes, and he's planted a lot of the grass there. He wrote letters in the 1950s complaining to his superiors in Bellingham, Washington, that they were planting European beach grass in areas where they shouldn't be planting.

"Some really bad mistakes were made early in dune stabilization," he says.

They sent the letters back to Ternyik with a note that said, "We don't want these kind of letters in our files. Don't send any more." So he kept planting.

Six steps remain. Wind whips around my shoes, scouring the hard-packed sand and carving pedestals under my feet. How quickly do I expect my presence to be erased? From where I stand, I see houses in the hills to the east. When the wind eases, I can hear cars on the highway. For the third time, I tell myself that this is a bad idea. It has been nearly an hour. The ridge is now smooth, and the six footprints are barely noticeable, just irregular bumps in the sand. But I know what they were, and it occurs to me that my presence in the wind may be preserving my prints. The last six may never blow away if I keep standing here, intruding on the natural order of shifting sand, like the grass. I stand staring without a break for several minutes, wishing them gone.

Then the wind gusts again and erases them. I am released. I move my feet and turn my back to the wind. I check my watch—an hour has passed since I stopped and stood. I want to put on a warm coat and stretch. I look at where my prints had been. Irregular bumps rise again. My prints, briefly buried, have resurfaced. My influence on the landscape is deeper than I assumed. Like the grass, I am not from here. But the longer I stay, the more my presence seems a part of this place.

Mark Blaine is editor of *Forest Magazine* and an adjunct faculty member of the University of Oregon School of Journalism and Communication. He's the author of *Whitewater: The Thrill and Skill of Running the World's Great Rivers* (Black Dog & Leventhal, 2001).

This essay was a finalist in the 2000 *Oregon Quarterly* Northwest Perspectives Essay Contest. It appeared in the Spring 2001 issue.

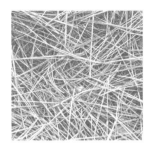

Grass Man

Charles Goodrich

Grass: democracy at its dumbest? Or utopian vegetation?

I am a grass man, I admit it. I love the plush look of a green lawn, the cush of grass underfoot. I love to smell it, touch it, sleep on it, make love on it. I like to lay on my belly in tall grass and watch insects climb through an architecture more intricate, more spired and cantilevered, more electric with predators and pitfalls than any celluloid space station. I like to play foolish music with a blade of grass till my lips tingle, then floss my teeth. I like to tickle my son's ear with grass. I like to suck the smidgen of sap from a stem.

And I like the mega-flora grasses even more. Kapa and I planted a clump of black bamboo outside our bedroom window and the stalks rustle like petticoats all night, toss calligraphic shadows on our ceiling at dawn. I'm a connoisseur of corn on the cob, and deeply dependent on wheat, rice and oats—grasses all. (Sugar cane, too.) I love grasses large and small, structural or edible, tuneful, whispery or mute. They say Lily Langtry loved to roll naked in the morning dew, and so do I.

But I hate to mow.

Jouncing over rugged ground on a little red riding mower, I'm decapitating the grass. The smelly tractor and I are what centaurs have devolved to, a sad confabulation of man and machine, fixated, not on anything sexy or magical, but on barbering the lawn. I wince with each bounce: the joint where my torso merges into machine is the thinned disc between the fifth lumbar and my iliacus. Down by the gear shift my sciatic nerve twitches in its ham.

The day, sunny and clear, is lovely—at least, out there it is, beyond my immediate atmosphere of clamor and chaff. My nose and eyes weep doggily. The noise is omnivorous, gobbling up the scoldings of scrub jays, the alarms of the crickets, the bright cries of Elliot and Jonah, my son and his best friend, waving to me from high in the apple tree. I sit up straight and salute them, sensing how they envy me. Seven-year-olds, they would mow in a minute. They would hybridize happily into boy-machines; the cartoons and comics they devour are full of such bionic heroes.

My neighbor's four Romney ewes stare at me through the wire fence. Their grass is browsed to the quick, so the smell of all this fresh hay, so close, so fragrant, and all going to waste makes their hair curl. Kapa and I have considered grazing sheep, too, but there are hassles galore in keeping livestock, starting with fences and ending with slaughter, and anyway, we don't really want to turn our grass into wool, or meat. Grass unto grass, we say. But that's a challenge.

Grass, generally speaking, is often low in the plant succession pecking order. Without intervention of some kind, shrubs and tree seedlings take root amid the grasses and gradually overtop them. Moderate grazing often favors the grass: The close clipping stimulates branching and fanning of blades, producing a denser, sturdier turf that resists invasion by woody species. But we didn't buy this acre to make like ungulates. We wanted a small orchard, a big garden, a place to hang a hammock. Kapa and I, it turns out, can thoroughly overwork ourselves gardening less than half an acre. On the other half, as sheepish Americans, we grow grass.

Chances are that this little swatch of ground, like much of the Willamette Valley, has been sprouting grass happily for 10,000 years. When the first Europeans—trappers and explorers, then missionaries and farmers—arrived here less than 200 years ago, they found the valley landscape dominated by open grasslands: wet prairie in the low areas where water stood in winter, dry prairie on the better-drained uplands. Oak forest held some of the hilly ground, and ash trees grew thick along the watercourses, but mostly the valley was grass—vast prairies of blue gramma, red fescue, tufted hair-grass, and nodding bent.

It took work to keep it that way. Our predecessors, the Kalapuya peoples of the valley, had their own set of reasons to favor grassy prairie—ease of passage, better browse for deer and other game animals, convenience of gathering staple foods like camas, tarweed and acorns. Perhaps, too, they enjoyed a sense of spaciousness. They didn't plow or mow or keep domestic cattle, but they did maintain most of the valley in an unforested state for ten millennia or so with one powerful tool: fire. Every fall, after the season's herbage browned out, the Kalapuya torched the prairie, burning much of the valley from today's Eugene to Portland.

When David Douglas, the plucky Scots botanist who gave his name to the Douglas-fir tree, rode through the valley in 1828, he complained repeatedly to his journal about the scorched countryside. "Country undulating; soil rich, light, with beautiful solitary oaks and pines interspersed through it… but… all burned and not a single blade of grass except on the margins of rivulets to be seen." Douglas inquired of the locals their reasons for burning. "Some of the natives tell me it is done for the purpose of urging the deer to frequent certain parts, to feed, which they leave unburned, and of course they are easily killed. Others say that it is done in order that they might the better find wild honey and grasshoppers…."

The practical advantages to the Kalapuya of burning the native prairies are evident. I wonder, though, about the actual event, the torching of the autumn fields. Was it an organized ritual, or just a routinized chore? I like to picture the older men and women reading the wind at dawn, arguing mildly over the relative humidity, divvying up the children and provisions and sending the families off to safety in the hills. Then the young men would run out along the margins of the prairie openings and with torches of pitchy fir ignite the grass.

The family groups would rest on the second ridge above the valley and watch the lines of fire slither along before the wind, the hanks of smoke rising and braiding together into heavy gray ropes. The changing season would be edged with sadness, but the fireworks below would excite and gladden them. Soon—after they'd gathered the acorns and the parched tarweed seed—they'd be moving into the hills for the duration of the rainy winter.

Elliot and I, on a hike through Finley Wildlife Refuge, watch from a hilltop as a convoy of huge combines swath across mile-wide fields down on the valley floor. Crows and turkey vultures flock to the small carrion left in their wake.

Out of the blue, Elliot asks, "Did buffalo used to live in the valley?"

"I don't think so. There's a herd of elk here in the Refuge, though."

"How old do you have to be to drive a combine?"

"Fourteen and three-quarters."

"Nah!"

"Really. I'll bet you some of the boys running those combines don't have a driver's license yet. I drove a combine when I was fourteen and three-quarters."

Across the valley, a giant column of smoke burls into the sky and flattens out into a bruise-colored cloud. After trucking the grain away, the farmers often burn their straw, torching the stubble with tractor-pulled flame-throwers, to rid the soil of fungus and diseases. Nearly 90 percent of the world's commercially-grown grass seed—ryes, fescues, clover, orchard grass—are produced in the Willamette Valley. It's exported around the globe, for lawns in Alaska, golf courses in Kuala Lumpur, pasture in the ashes of the Bolivian rain forest. Grass seed is one of the staple crops of our regional agriculture. We are a people fattened on grass.

Some observers have suggested that we are also flattened by our grass. Michael Pollan has written, "With our open-faced front lawns we declare our like-mindedness to our neighbors.... We are all property owners here, the lawn announces...." The demographics of grass express a collective attitude to landscape, a preference for the uniform and the plain, bordering on the mono-maniacal, and heavily dependent on technology— machinery and agricultural chemicals—to maintain the lawn in an undynamic limbo.

The lawn serves as a slavish foreground to the house, its horizontal plainness accentuating the building's angles and ornament. And grass may act as a visual moat around the house, an open space that strangers must negotiate, where no miscreant can hide. Snooty neighborhoods can be tyrannical about grass—let yours get weedy or tall, let it brown out, unwatered, in July, and you will feel the heat from your neighbors.

A few years ago, Kapa and I considered torching our backyard. Fire, we knew, was the finest tool for maintaining a landscape in grass, but burning our lawn would have raised eyebrows among the neighbors. So we decided to resign from the lawn-scape and go prairie.

"We'll just let it grow!" we said, delighted by our audacity.

And it was beautiful. Beyond the persimmon tree began something like a native place, the grasses stretching taller and taller. We ogled the graceful weave of subtly hued colors, the seed-heads waving in the evening breeze. It was easy to believe reports of the munificence of the aboriginal prairies, of horses wading to the shoulder in a sea of grass.

Elliot and his friends loved to make tunnels through the arching grain, to creep and spy on Kapa and me working in the garden. They'd pop up and holler, "Woo-hoo!" and duck down and giggle hysterically.

It seemed there were more good insects around that summer, and more swallows and bats, too. Why did we ever mow?

Then came the letter from the fire marshal, polite but emphatic. It said, in effect, all grass will be mowed to a height no greater than eight inches after the first of July. Comply, comply, comply. The clerk I phoned at the fire department pleasantly told me that the ordinance was cut and dry—either mow, or the city would mow for us and send us the bill.

It was a small grief, but we went through all the classic stages—anger, denial, begrudging acceptance. Still, we hemmed and hawed. A day of heavy showers reduced the potential for fire, and we didn't think the city would press its ordinance in the absence of real danger. Then another hard rain dragged down much of the grass, and the prairie began to look kind of ragged. The kids quit hiding in the flattened grass, preferring to kick the soccer ball in the neighbor's neatly clipped side yard.

Finally in late July, after hot dry weather had returned, and the parched grasses, in full-headed ripeness, lifted up and waved once again in a late evening breeze, I resigned myself to the mowing. I rented a tractor with a brush hog, then took one last loving stroll through the rustling prairie, sighing over the delicate sweeps of color—the pale ochres, siennas and rusts—stroking the swollen seed-heads. Then I noticed a knee-high Nootka rose bush sprawling amid the grasses, and then another, and another, and here and there stout clumps of Himalayan blackberry, and lots of vicious little hawthorn trees.

It was natural succession, and it was taking over our backyard! Succession, not into a picturesque natural woodland, not into maples or oaks, or even Douglas-firs—no, a thicket of thorns and brambles was sprouting up under my feet! For the first time I felt that diesel tractor idling behind me as, not an evil implement, but a trusty ally. I mowed with new purpose, the beautiful grasses just collateral casualties in a battle against nature barbed and shameless.

Last mow of the season, chopping down the brown stubble before the autumn rains begin—which will happen tomorrow, according to the weatherman. A fleet of battleship-gray clouds steams past Marys Peak, ominously punctual.

Elliot's riding in my lap, steering. He is simply awe struck by the mower's eleven horsepower, so proud of this borrowed force that he's over-steering, weaving back and forth in his ardor to master it. He shivers like a pony, his spirit prancing.

My spirit is conflicted, caught in the intersection between grass and gasoline. I want to help Elliot be competent to the demands of the world, but what if some of those demands are misleading and unsustainable? I hope he outgrows his fascination with machines faster than the grass over-takes our streets when the gas is gone. At Elliot's school the other day, I heard the councilor use a deft phrase, telling the mother of a disruptive child, "I believe you've over-empowered him." And I thought, yeah, we're an over-empowered culture, aren't we? If this mower ride is a sort of an initiation for Elliot, it's a bogus one, an initiation into a sham society of ill-spent power. I hug him close, for safety, and nudge back slightly on the throttle.

But at the same time, he is so excited, so pulled-forward into life that he trembles with energy, humming snatches of "Yankee Doodle," bouncing in my lap, an ecstatic young animal. He loves me for giving him this opportunity, this trust, this enormous power. I'll be his hero at least until supper.

Grass is so unprepossessing it lends itself to vast manipulation as readily as wild imagining. Grass may bring out in us some impulse toward hege-mony, blandness and conformity; it may be democracy at its dumbest. Or it may be the archetype of generosity and creativity, a utopian vegetation.

Live grass is green fire, a cool combustion, sunlight slow-cooking carbon and spice into shoots and roots. I kiss Elliot on the cheek, he climbs down, and I grind the transmission into a higher gear. Gotta get this job done in time to make supper. The swallows are out, zinging through the air all around me, snatching the bugs stirred up by the mower. My back aches and my hands smell of gas, reminding me of William Burroughs' spooky name for our age, the "gasoline crack of history," and in my fatigue I'm treated to one of those flashes of spurious omniscience: I see myself grazing along with all the herbivores throughout the ages, a minuscule glint of metal and flesh, moving like a beast over a tiny field of green.

Charles Goodrich's first full-length collection of poetry, *Insects of South Corvallis,* will be published in 2003 by Cloudbank Books. He worked for twenty-five years as a professional gardener and is presently retooling to become an elementary school teacher.

This essay won second place in the 2002 *Oregon Quarterly* Northwest Perspectives Essay Contest.

Blood Relation

Bobbie Willis

Battling blackberries, a writer finds a kind of wild.

I have a scar high up on the inside of my left forearm. You could miss it, smooth and faint as it is. But I know it's there—maybe two inches long—carved cleanly and swiftly with Ginsu precision.

The scar came from a fight I got into a couple summers ago. I fared pretty badly, bleeding from my forearm as well as from scratches on the outside of my left leg.

I could almost hear the announcer: *The winner and champeeeeen: Rubus fruticosus*—one mean, wild blackberry bramble. Naively, I fought the bramble with hedge clippers, snapping the wooden handles together in clenched fists: *Swacka-click-swacka* hissed the blades as they scissored into my tangled defeat.

I grew up in Southern California on Felinda Way, a cul-de-sac pinching off of bustling Olive Avenue. This was the safe pocket in which my parents chose to settle and start a family after moving from their island home in the South Pacific. Across Olive was the space I considered wild—an expanse of rolling, dusty hills covered in dry grass that shines golden now in my mind. It's what I picture when I sing "…amber waves of grain." My younger brother Mark and I would beg permission to cross the avenue, to walk that open space in the name of exploration and freedom.

We'd wind along the dirt path carved through the grass, looking for gopher holes and listening for snakes. Mark usually found a stick to whip and switch through the air. Sometimes in the taller patches of grass we'd find abandoned washing machines or other giant appliances. Sometimes we'd find garbage sacks, neither of us brave enough to break them open. "What if it's a body?" Mark always asked. Once we found an old mattress and box spring, and we spent the afternoon jumping on it, higher and higher, feeling free and wild as children reared by wolves.

But it was otherwise rare for us to question our suburban boundaries. We took piano lessons and played Pop Warner football. We ate tuna casserole and chicken casserole and good old American meatloaf—our favorite. Our snacks came mostly from the supermarket: Florida oranges, Washington apples, Chiquita bananas. Every summer my dad would bring home a huge sack of cherries, and this we considered exotic—our fruit extravaganza. Mark and I would eat and spit until we were sick to our stomachs. While we knew this as exotic food, we had no concept of *wild* food—the kind you could just find and eat right off the vine.

My parents knew this sort of food before they moved to California. I remember my dad telling us how as a boy he would shin up the trunk of a palm tree to pluck a sweet, green *niu*—a just-ripe coconut, whose juice tingled and fizzed like ginger ale. He'd tell us how the *esi,* or papaya, grew to be bigger than his head. It made him laugh to see these stateside papayas, barely bigger than lemons, stacked neatly in the fruit bins at Safeway.

My parents grew up in such intimate proximity to nature that it wove itself into their daily chores, their weekly routines, their legends and lore. They told us stories of spurned and broken-hearted lovers who settled in a spot to cry away their anguish; and there they were transformed, fixed forever as taro, papaya, coconut, guava. My parents' wild home lent itself to mythology in a way my suburbia-sown childhood did not.

As a grownup, I've moved northward, up into the Willamette Valley. This valley kills me a little every spring and summer—it's the grass seed and Scotch broom pollen mostly that do it. People here who have allergies like to say Native Americans called the region "Valley of Sickness" or "Valley of Death." They did in fact use these terms, but endearingly so: This valley was a place to send the sick and dying so that they could be rejuvenated, inspired by lush and wild life to recuperate and live again.

Of course, to me it seems particularly lush and wild given the avenues and cul-de-sacs of my past. Nature—the notion of it I dreamed as a child—hangs around closer to home: There's a young buck that gallops through a front yard with an arrow hanging from the scarred-over hole in his side. There are blue jays with cheeky blue Mohawk crowns. There are wild strawberries and salmonberries and thimbleberries just waiting to be plucked and eaten. It's all in such intimate proximity—my own wild and natural world.

The Coast Salish have chronicled this natural world through stories like the ones I learned from my parents. This tribe tells of a jealous husband who chases his wife up into a thorny tree. The thorns cut the woman. Her blood falls from the tree and becomes blackberry.

Come late summer there are blackberries everywhere around here—insinuating themselves along the banks of Amazon Creek, looming in the shadows along the McKenzie River, cozying up to the edges of the grass seed farms in Junction City, Tangent, Halsey. You blink, and a tendril becomes a tentacle; a bud becomes a bloom, becomes a fat, black berry. The whole thing takes on a dark and quiet lushness—a voluptuous, even mildly seductive, display.

Seductive enough, in fact, that when I moved into a brick-covered duplex with nasturtium and hardy fuchsia at the back step and just a few shoots of blackberry outside the bedroom window, my first thought was, "Blackberry cobbler." It was April. I figured I could keep those shoots under control until August; and there I'd be with the mother lode of black gold.

Blackberries have an ancestral line as long and circuitous as their own tangled physique. Some say the plants originated in Asia, though others argue for origins in the Middle East. After a stint in Europe, the plants worked their way to the Americas as a food source. Archaeological finds in Scandinavia indicate blackberries were eaten by the Vikings.

The blackberry's survival has to do with seeds, physiology and geography. The plants produce a huge quantity of seeds, which birds eat and distribute in their droppings. This alone makes it virtually impossible to eliminate the plants. But just in case, blackberry stalks, which can grow to twenty-five feet, preserve themselves twofold by taking root wherever the stalks touch ground.

The blackberry's underground network is made up of rhizomes—thick, fibrous structures similar to knots of ginger root. The rhizome design makes the blackberry one seriously efficient plant machine. While the green parts grow and spread above ground, the rhizomes work underground to put out roots—many, many roots. These roots mature to become new rhizomes. These rhizomes create new shoots, which take in water and sunlight to feed the systems down below, which then create more roots and rhizomes and so on. Given the right cocktail of sunlight, water and food, the rate of propagation can be staggering. And the Willamette Valley has just what the blackberry ordered: acidic soil (heavy on the clay), high moisture and sufficient periods of hot sunlight. As the stalks grow, flop over, touch ground, root—then grow and touch ground again—a few shoots can turn into a tangled and unwieldy bramble in no time.

By the beginning of July, my nest of blackberry shoots had grown to the gutter along the edge of the roof, blocking the view through my bedroom window. The tops of the stalks curved back down toward the ground, hanging dangerously in the path of the back walkway. That thicket looked gruesome, yet oddly gorgeous—a monster that would reach out to tickle your chin just before slashing your throat. My neighbors said nothing, but I caught them keeping their distance. When for three days in a row, my hair, backpack and T-shirt got caught on the thorns of overhanging stems, I decided it was time to do some trimming.

Blackberries have a willful streak. They careen easily out of control and choke out all competing plant life. You can rein them in, or perhaps round them up, with pesticides such as Roundup. Roundup is part of a family of chemicals called glyphosates. These chemicals, touted for their biodegradability, work as "leaf foliants." This is fancy for saying that the pesticide disrupts the way the leaves absorb sunlight. The plant can't convert sunlight to food, so it withers and dies, sometimes within just a week or two of spraying.

I've seen thickets of sprayed blackberry bushes, and they're spooky: The plants turn a true black—dull and dried out. The berry clusters hang like tiny shrunken heads. It makes me want to stop picking, makes me want to go home and wash my whole self in a hot, soapy shower.

Blackberry bushes can also be managed with simple elbow grease. Washington State University's Regional Garden Column recommends: "Digging out these weeds by shovel or mattock, getting as much of the root system as possible, gives a good start on management. If a large acreage must be cleared…rent a bulldozer."

I didn't even own hedge clippers, so I had to borrow some from friends. I knew enough to wear gloves, but I didn't bother to change out of my Saturday afternoon tank top and shorts. And this, along with a box of plastic kitchen trash bags, was how I armed myself.

Stalks of blackberry thorns are like rows of shark's teeth: They go on forever, and every last one of them—from the giant granddaddy thorns, to the newest pinpoints—will carve an exposed arm or leg like it was last Sunday's chicken dinner.

Around eleven o'clock that July morning, I stepped up to the bramble—it was probably four feet across and twelve or fifteen feet high at the tallest stem. I poked the clippers in, moved the two biggest stalks to the right, and I cut one of them low, down near the base of the thicket.

Now this was not so smart. The stalk was at least two inches around and the hedge clippers were about as effective as those safety scissors from grade school. (I learned later that you want a smaller tool—something snippy and maneuverable and sharp—to get right in and snap through the woody stems.)

When the clippers failed, I started pulling at the plant—bending the stem back and forth, hoping to tear it away. Again, I put the blades to the cut I had made, scissored furiously at it and finally broke through.

That's when the whole stalk fell on top of me.

I battled that thicket all the hot afternoon and had four sloppy plastic trash bags of clippings to show for it. The blackberries had caught and stretched the plastic on its thorns, and it all looked very suspicious, like something from a horror movie breaking out for the last attack scene.

I was bleeding. Most of the exposed skin on my left side had caught that first fallen stalk. I had a small scratch on my cheekbone, one on my collarbone, a whole series along the outside of my thigh and calf. And, of course, there was the cut on my forearm. That was a deep one. It showed me who was boss.

When I stepped back to take a look at my work, I was dumbfounded. I'd gotten rid of the tallest three or four stems, and I had clipped and clipped deep into the heart of the bramble. But to look at it, it was as though I had accomplished nothing—as though maybe the whole thing was growing precisely as fast as I was trimming it.

Nothing ever did come of the berries in that bramble. Turns out it didn't get enough direct sunlight to sweeten anything within reach. The landlady eventually hired landscapers to come in and till the whole patch. Two years later when I moved out, new shoots were already back.

Blackberries have redeeming qualities. Native Americans used them for all sorts of things: The fruit could cure canker sores in the mouth; a tea brewed from the dried leaves could calm a troubled stomach; the young shoots could be peeled, boiled and eaten as a vegetable. The Salish used the stems to scrub a person's body as part of a purification rite before spirit dancing.

Last September, in the purple-blue light that comes just after sunset, I went blackberry picking along Amazon Creek. If you cover up your arms with long sleeves, you can pick the best berries deep in the heart of the bramble. I filled my biggest Rubbermaid tub, the weight of the berries at the top crushing the poor berries at the bottom. One rule for ripeness is to pick fruit that feels heavier than it looks. My tub of berries was *heavy*, filled as it was with the trophies of summer sunshine, spring showers and the soil that waits in winter to let those stalks take hold and shoot boldly into the world.

I use blackberries for cobbler: Cook a quart of berries to boiling. Melt a stick of butter in a Pyrex baking dish. Mix together a cup of flour, a cup of sugar, 3 teaspoons of baking powder, and a cup of milk. Pour this batter over the butter and the berries over the batter. Bake it all for half an hour at 350 degrees. The cake will rise to the surface, making a tender crust to cover that thick, sweet-tangy mess of blackberry goodness. Your house will smell like the inside of a birthday cake. Eat the cobbler with Umpqua vanilla ice cream, and try not to let your tears of joy water down the dessert too much.

This Northwest is my wild, where I learn again and again the lines defining nature and not-nature. I give in to things that are a part of *the* world, if not necessarily part of my world. Sometimes the slugs win. Sometimes the pollen tortures you. Sometimes the deer get every rose in the garden and the blackberries cut you to pieces.

I'd like to think that if humanity burns itself out on concrete and Styrofoam peanuts, that the world will be left to cover herself as wildly as she pleases: in bright yellow swatches of Scotch broom and dandelions; in prickly, sweet blackberries that grow to the moon.

There's something about this wild profusion and excess I admire— something about it that speaks to my own nature. Sometimes you just find the right home. You find what you need. You grow and live. You flourish.

Bobbie Willis is a writer. Her projects include staff work for *Eugene Weekly*, as well as a memoir and various essays. She was the recipient of an Oregon Literary Arts fellowship in 2003.

This essay won third place in the 2002 *Oregon Quarterly* Northwest Perspectives Essay Contest.

Fire Ban

Ana Maria Spagna

Friends gather in a dry season, eager for fire.

The night is unusually dry along the Columbia Gorge. Rain gear had remained wadded in our packs all day. Dead limbs snapped under our boots. By late afternoon, the wind blew in an ominous haze, too flat and formless to rightly be called clouds. If this were summer, if we were at work, radios would crackle an alert for extreme fire danger. But it is not summer, and we are not at work, not paid at least. We are at Stewman's helping him, ironically as it turns out, to reduce fire hazard on his property.

Stewman owns five acres in a community chock-full of alternative-lifestyle fixtures: hay bale homes and solar panels, vegetable gardens and libertarian politics. In terms of eccentricity, he fits right in. As a boy, he flew on the circus trapeze and was featured in the *Saturday Evening Post.* He once had a booth at the Oregon Country Fair where he sold bowls of stew. Hence the nickname. He is a licensed ham radio operator (even now, in these webbish days) with a painfully sweet tenor voice. He is, in short, a man of many talents, many friends and not much cash. So, he invited a crowd to camp for the weekend and do some work in exchange for a song, a beer and a bowl of the namesake stew. And, we presumed, a campfire.

We arrived late in the morning, straggling in groggily, armed with mini-mart coffee and chainsaws. Then we got to work, felling some of his small-diameter trees in one swift kerf, yanking them free of the limby thicket overhead, leaving a more open mosaic of fir and pine and oak. This kind of thinning, foresters say, reduces the threat of a crown fire, the scariest kind of fire, one that leaps from treetop to treetop lickety-split without ever touching the ground. So we bucked the downed trees into stovewood lengths and chucked the limbs high onto Volkswagen-sized heaps for Stewman to burn later in the winter when the danger won't be so high. Most of us do something like this for a living, and all of us are at least part-time firefighters, so the day went smoothly enough. Now, as darkness prods us out of the woods, there is just one glitch. Due to the dryness, a countywide fire ban is in effect.

That leaves Stewman more than a little nervous. In this crowd, he knows what's coming. We fidget on the hay bales arranged in a circle for the occasion, a little too quiet, too somber. Stewman pulls out his plug-in campfire gag, a rotisserie of aluminum foil illuminated by an orange light bulb, and that proves good for a courtesy laugh, but not much use for keeping twenty people warm in a late October windstorm. Finally, despite the wind, despite the law, some of Stewman's guests begin piling pinecones in the center of the circle. Then they go looking for a match.

It's becoming common knowledge that the problem in the woods isn't what Smokey led us to believe—that we're burning them down—but the fact that for a hundred years we haven't let them burn. That's why beetles gnaw away whole stands, scientists argue, why invasive species nudge out natives, why second-growth forests choke themselves off from sunlight. That's also why the nightly news superlatives come in too-frequent waves:

1988 was the worst fire season in 100 years! 1994 was the worst fire season in 100 years! 2000 was…. Nearly everyone agrees that the solution is to start prescribed fires, fires with predetermined parameters in terms of geography, weather and available resources, fires that in principle provide all the nifty benefits with none of the terror. The result is that, these days, a firefighter's job involves a fair bit of schizophrenia: now start a fire; now put it out. Not that it bothers any of the firefighters I know. As long as something's on fire, they're happy.

Seasonal firefighters get hired on early in the spring and pace around the cache—where fire tools are stored and firefighters report to work each morning—waiting for the chance to burn. Occasionally, when they are short-handed, I'll help out. I'll lug a pair of drip torches, canisters of gasoline-and-diesel mix with elaborate golfball-sized wicks, into the forest still patchy with snow. The crew boss will line us out with military precision to begin walking slowly (More slowly! he'll bark), dribbling flame from the torch wicks. Sometimes, when the humidity drops at around eleven in the morning, the fire starts. Flames travel in procession, then arc away along contours of the land, and eventually, with some luck, take off willy-nilly to torch a few fire-starved Ponderosas or diseased firs. Other times there is no luck. We'll trickle gallons of fuel into the earth and leave only a few squiggly black lines across soggy leaves. It's dirty, smelly work, and it is unspeakably frustrating. That's half the reason, I'll tell myself, that I'm not a full-time firefighter: too much ado about nothing.

At least that's how it can seem. One season I did work in fire full time, but only because I was injured, and then only as a dispatcher. I sat in the office surrounded by firefighters ever hopeful for the big one—a raging wildfire in Montana or Arizona, say, full of danger and drama and the chance for the big bucks. When a fire call did come, the power struggle over who would be sent was so intense that I began to beg to go on fires myself. When I did, I would sit in fire camp and fill out timesheets for three hours, then collect overtime for nine or eleven more hours. I wore my sandals in protest against the whole embarrassing extravaganza. Fire, it seemed, was a big game, a farce, deserving of my disdain. Where are your fire boots? the Incident Commander demanded. These are them, I said, my sandaled feet crossed in plain view.

It's just a fire, I thought. Gawd.

Firefighters or not, those of us who live and work in the rural Northwest lead lives marked by fire. We heat with wood in winter, waking in the morning to kneel by the woodstove, lay out kindling, and blow gently on the coals. We burn slash in spring, hauling brush in the rain as evening descends, whole armloads of needles, so pungent, sticking to our faces like camouflage. And in summer, we have campfires. We grill oysters and salmon and watch the stars, swathed occasionally in the eerie green of the northern lights, and play music.

We have our instruments—guitars, mandolins, harmonicas—out of their worn cases, cradled in pitch-stained palms when Stewman begins to beg.

"The fine will be upwards of a thousand dollars," he pleads.

"We'll put it out. We'll put it out," the firefighters promise.

One year, not too long after my summer in the fire office, the big one came to us. A lightning storm hit after two months of drought, and while others laid hose lines, the crew boss sent me up a knoll to be a lookout. For a week, I watched the fire loiter, unmoving, near a ridge top until suddenly the wind would shift or an ember would roll into new fuel, and the fire would leap a few acres in seconds and settle in place for hours. I had lots of free time. I wrote long letters on the backs of maps. I listened to helicopters dropping their buckets into the lake and watched ash settling like snow over the valley below. One morning, weather specialists announced that the fire would reach the inhabited valley floor that day. It was a certainty, they predicted: the destruction, the nightly news drama, homes in ashes, the freight train roar charging down the mountainside, fast and sure as the flare-ups I'd watched with cool detachment from above. There was fear in the air, yes, but more than a hint of adrenaline beneath the surface. (Yes, yes, let it come, like the heated moments of sex.) The fire never came, but it was close. Danger and drama passed like so many miles of unused hose.

Before the fateful match is struck, Stewman gets an idea. He herds the fire-crazed crowd into a small shed; they emerge squealing with delight. They assemble an iron barrel stove in the center of the party, stack the stovepipe three sections high, and start a modest fire. It is not an open fire, so it is technically legal, and it is certainly safer. Stewman plucks his guitar and croons campfire standards, including a version of "Mr. Bojangles" with new lyrics dedicated to a mean-spirited ranger who was known as a particularly vicious enforcer of firewood collection permits.

As Stewman sings, more and more small logs are stuffed into the stove until the black iron glows red. Eventually, if this were an open fire, some-one would begin heaving more rounds—bigger logs! longer ones!—into the fire, sending sparks flittering, branding souvenir scabs onto fleece jackets, singeing eyebrows. The barrel stove has done little to dampen the enthu-siasm. Soon flames are spewing geyser-like out the top pipe, eager and rambunctious. And the crowd is cheering.

This is how I know the allure of fire runs deeper than whether it's good for the land or bad: My friends are crazy for fire. They watch thunderheads build, and they are charged, electrified, off in search of their binoculars and their boots. They stand watching a slash unit ignite into a whirling column of flame, and they surge forward against the wind, wanting to get closer, to be a part of it. When called upon, their exuberance can become heroic. I tell myself that maybe I could be heroic too, if it came to that. There are fewer experienced full-time firefighters these days and, hence, more demand for experienced part-timers like me. I follow orders well, and I've been fighting fire long enough, if occasionally reluctantly, to have some skill. Still, I watch the antics, then back away. I lack the passion. That's the other half-reason, I might as well admit, that I'm not a full-time firefighter.

It's not exactly fear. I am more frightened of driving in city traffic or of flying over the ocean than I am of fire. Fire is familiar, and if not exactly predictable, at least visceral, real and close. If it's not under my control, it's at least not under anyone else's control. That's where my distrust comes in. It's not fire itself that bothers me. It's when people mess around with it. That's what worries me about this whole post-Smokey quandary. If our relationship with nature, like our relationships with each other, is a balancing act, then fire is the most extreme case in point. If we don't start fires, fire might engulf us. If we start fires, fire might engulf us. We must burn a little bit, or let it burn. Just the right amount at just the right time. No matter what. The relationship between us and fire is terrifying and seductive and imperative. All too often it seems impossible.

But not at Stewman's. Out here on the scrubby fringe, anything is possible, even perfect equilibrium. The embers spiral higher and higher and threaten to ignite the tinder-dry fir needles overhead. Just before they do, Stewman returns to the shed and emerges triumphantly flaunting a fourth section of stovepipe. He dons leather gloves and stands on his tiptoes to slide the new section over the inferno, capping the fire temporarily, taming it for now.

Eventually the excitement subsides. I sit next to Stewman, who has set aside his guitar. The fire has brought out his melancholy sure as a minor chord, and I am afraid he will start lamenting his last girlfriend, a girl so young and wild he never should have believed she would stay.

Turns out, when the big one came, it burned a valley that had been Stewman's favorite hiking destination. I told him the summer after the girlfriend left how beautiful the trail had become after the fire. Tiny blades of grass sprouted under blackened ancient pines. Pink fireweed swayed in the wind, as tall as corn stalks. Everything, I told him, is beginning anew. Stewman shouldered his pack and plodded up the trail. Upon his return he told me, in no uncertain terms, that he did not find it beautiful and that he would never return. The valley was dead, charred, ruined, he said. I felt sorry for recommending the hike and wondered if I had been brainwashed by the fire-is-good zealots, or if my own place in life—years removed from the last heartbreak—skewed my aesthetics.

I remember my mistake by the barrel stove and vow to be sympathetic if the girlfriend comes up, but she does not. Instead, Stewman grows sentimental. "I got the cream of the crop," he says, meaning the twenty of us who showed up out of more than a hundred he invited. "The best of the best."

I lean in close, give him a one-armed hug, and leave to seek refuge in the back of my pickup. I lie awake, listening to the canopy shift and whine in the wind and thinking about fire. No matter how I bristle, over time, fire becomes more a part of living in the Northwest: because there are more fires, because there are fewer firefighters, because more of us have migrated closer to the fire-starved woods and we have more to lose. At the same time, as fire danger grows exponentially and air-quality laws become more stringent, fire bans necessarily become more frequent. It might not be long, some of my neighbors worry, before we aren't allowed to have fires at all. No woodstoves, no brush burning, no campfires. If we regulate fires, then only regulators will have fires, they say. Maybe they are right. And if it happens, despite everything, I think we will have lost touch with something. Something, well, elemental.

In the morning Stewman appears, freshly showered, in khaki pants and suspenders and a fine new felt hat. The wind has died down, and the sun illuminates Mt. Hood, fiery orange and alpenglow pink. Stewman begins frying eggs one at a time on a hot plate, and most of us are content with coffee while we wait. But a few diehards cannot help themselves. They slough away, swiping limbs from atop yesterday's tidy piles, snapping them over their knees, then lingering by the barrel stove, blowing on their fingers, laying kindling, trying to strike a match to start a morning fire. (Again! again! they clap like two-year-olds.) And everything begins anew.

Ana Maria Spagna lives in Stehekin, Washington. She works on a National Park Service trail crew and writes. Her work has appeared in *Orion, Utne Reader, Open Spaces, Cimarron Review, West Wind Review* and elsewhere.

This essay was the winner of the 2002 *Oregon Quarterly* Northwest Perspectives Essay Contest. It appeared in the Summer 2002 issue of *Oregon Quarterly*.

The Way We Mourn

Gayle Forman

Processing loss, finding wisdom.

February 8, 2001, started out as an unusual morning. A light snow had fallen in northwest Oregon, not enough for snowmen but enough to wet the roads and to close schools. At about 1:30 that afternoon, two cars collided along Highway 31 on a stretch of the curvy two-lane road that runs from Clatskanie west to the coast. And as happens every day, people died. But as doesn't happen every day, the crash killed an entire family who were my good friends the Christies—Robert, Denise, Ted and John, ages thirty-five, thirty-five, eight and one, respectively.

Newspaper accounts reported that "a Clatskanie family was killed," a terse explanation that seemed wholly insufficient and surprisingly insulting now that I was the one living the tragedy, not writing about it. For starters, they were a Eugene family at heart. Robert and Denise were both University of Oregon grads. They were married atop the town's City Hall; their sons, Ted and John, were born at Sacred Heart. Eugene was where they planted gardens, played in bands, planned for futures now truncated. The family had only left Eugene last August when Robert, with teaching certificate fresh in hand, was hired at Clatskanie High School.

But even if the papers had tagged them a Eugene family, that would've rankled me. Somehow attaching their life to a location belied the profound effect these people had on those of us who knew them. No newspaper article, nor even this essay, can fully communicate how special they were. But what comes closest to describing these remarkable people is the way we mourned them.

Within a few days of the Christies' deaths, and without any formal planning or discussion, a group of the family's close friends, who had not all been together in years, descended from various points in the country upon the house of Greg and Diane Rios, the remaining Eugene contingent of our now scattered community. Upon hearing the horrific news, we'd each found our way to Eugene, lured by some invisible pull.

On Thirteenth Street, once ground-zero for the Eugene bohemian scene to which this group all belonged, Joe, a bearded giant from Salem shuffled aimlessly until he bumped into Mike, a gaunt musician from Seattle, who in turn steered the duo to Greg's office whereupon Greg drove the lost souls back to his home. There, the rest of us were waiting—a diverse assembling of suburban parents, New York City journalists, Olympia artists, a Eugene chef, a lesbian-mommed family. Each of us had brought with us hastily packed bags full of mementos: old pictures, letters, e-mails, short stories, set-lists from now defunct bands, drum sticks. These artifacts, along with the stories we told, sketched a picture of the Christies' lives.

Of course, we were simply partaking in ancient rituals of mourning. But that this ad hoc wake had happened so spontaneously and that the dozen or so people who showed up, each of us with vastly different lives, had all arrived at the same destination, with the same impulses, was both surprising and consoling.

We live in a bizarrely disconnected and conflicted world, one in which, I believe, it is still thought that unhappiness is something best kept private. We step gingerly around tragedy, not wanting to poke too far and increase the pain. I knew that mourning was a team sport but having never lost anyone except for grandparents and distant friends, I merely thought that the point of grieving among friends was to have some company for my misery.

Like all things connected to this tragedy, the truth was more profound. Not only did everyone seem to have the same common impulses around these deaths, we all seemed to be grappling with similar spiritual issues. As we were licking wounds and rushing headlong into the hell of our loss, we found something there that looked a little like wisdom. From within the depth of our grief, many of us felt a sense of being part of something divine. Not visited in an Oprah-angels-are-watching-us sense. Rather, in the swirl of sadness and horror, we felt a clarity, a guidance, a moral compass.

What was this? Was this God? Was this our newly departed friends watching out for us? How would this tragedy change us? How would we change us? How would we rise to the occasion—not just of their deaths but of our lives? I was dumbfounded by the similarity in our spiritual fumblings, by the sameness of our questions. If this accident had given me a disquieting glimpse of the randomness of life, it had also given me an even rarer glimpse of the deeper meaning of community.

I had thought this common group reaction was particular to us, the mourners of the Family Christie. Then, a month after the accident, I read a book called *Hard Travel to Sacred Places* by Rudolph Wurlitzer, who writes about traveling in the post-devastation haze after his wife's twenty-one-year-old son was killed in a car crash. He writes: "I feel compelled to push toward the margins of my 'aloneness,' to give in to alienation, exhaustion, and grief, not to mention the odd unexpected moment of wonder, because grief, as I have been learning, along with everything else it brings, can sometimes shatter ordinary self-absorption and vanity with such force that, for a moment, it seems to set one free."

It was the most perfect and succinct description of the heady emotions we were all dealing with. And it made me realize that the community of the grieving transcends me, my friends, my family. We all strive to be special, to prove the validity of our individual feelings, but in this sense, the fact that Rudy Wurlitzer understands my deepest sadness, and that I understand that of someone I've never met, makes me feel connected to

Gayle Forman

other people in a way I rarely experience. The Christies were the center of community for so many different people. Their deaths have fused each of us to one another and to a larger unknown community. To me, this more than anything shows the indelible influence these four wonderful people had—will continue to have—on the lives of those who loved them.

■

Gayle Forman is a journalist living in New York City. Contributions for a memorial fund set up to honor the Christies can be sent to the Robert Christie Family Scholarship, Astoria High School, 1636 Irving Avenue, Astoria, OR 97103.

This essay appeared in the Summer 2001 issue of *Oregon Quarterly*.

Salmon Run

Bette Lynch Husted

Healing wounds of loss and history.

Sometimes breathing is the hardest part. I am so numb I forget how, I can't remember why. Sometimes—these are the worst times, and the easiest—I'm just angry, so angry I look at the faces of the men in my prison class who are up for murder and think: *my cousins, my kinsmen.* I understand the shapes of the penciled letters on their two allotted sheets of paper. These are the days when blame sprays in my wake like wood chips from the Potlatch chip trucks, blasting the windshield of anyone behind me, arcing out over the banks. It's all part of the same story, I think on those days. The juvenile officer with the nine-inch stack of case folders on his desk, the mental health counselors and hospital reception- ists and Children's Services workers, the people who promised help and then said no, they couldn't give it, how had we possibly gotten the idea that they could? The treatment center that wouldn't let him back in because he had run away, the caseworker with the leather face on the other side of the table who told him, "You'll be out on the street in a few weeks and dead within a year. You might as well kill yourself and get it over with. Get out of our hair right now."

"If there are no salmon to eat, let them eat something else," I hear Floyd Dominy say on television one night. Bureau of Reclamation. Human Services. The television documentary switches to black and white, the last dip-netting at Celilo, which the narrator mispronounces Ce-LEE-lo: "A vanishing fish for a vanishing race." "I promise you," I had said to the leather-faced man, my voice shaking (how do these words sound to my son, sitting there in his too-short Juvie sweatpants and the ripped orange T-shirt? Does he see me looking for the mark on his neck?)—"you think you don't care, but if he dies, I will make sure that you regret it, too."

The angry days are the easiest, days when my hatred obliterates this chain of gray-white faces as if they were on TV with Floyd Dominy, click, off. Easiest because, of course, the face I really want to disappear is the one that startles me above the bathroom sink in the middle of the night and ambushes me from the blank glare of store windows. The face that my son, in the dream where the boy in the convertible is really him, his hair longer now but those are his ears, his shoulders—I am already reaching to touch his cheek—the face that he turns to see, that makes his mouth twist into panic, shouting (mouth dissolving like a smoke ring) to the driver, "Go! Go! Get out of here!" The face that, in refusing to let him die, has driven him away. *A hospital? A lockup hospital?* The face he is afraid of.

I would be different, I had told myself as a child. I would keep trying to hear the voices of the spirits that whispered in the pine needles. I would remember that grasses spoke and ravens. April coyotes in the draw. I would live quietly, listening. When I grew up, there would be no more family quarrels, no more separation of mothers and sons.

But my son is gone. The voices I hear now are telling the story of Colonel Pratt and the boarding schools. A program on public television. *Kill the Indian and save the man.* I study the photograph of Pratt's supporters, the Friends of the Indian, gathered in the banquet hall to balance the savage force let loose by Sheridan, by Sherman and Custer. Their faces shine. I know a piece of something now that Colonel Pratt and the Friends of the Indian didn't learn: the price of good intentions.

He's been gone for almost two summers when Dean and I drive back up the highway to the lake where our son's life spark began. We want to sleep again in the mountains of Montana. A full moon follows us across the night, piercing my chest through the branches of the lodgepoles until I think no, this cannot be borne. At daybreak we follow the Going to the Sun highway over the backbone of the world and down into Browning. On the bench outside the general store a man waits to trade a stag-handled hunting knife for more wine. "Go on home now, Raymond," the clerk tells him. He leans over him, pointing up the street, but he doesn't touch him. "G'mornin'," the man says to us, putting the knife back into his pocket. He hunches his shoulders in his dirty nylon vest. The temperature has fallen forty degrees; behind us, in the mountains, two feet of snow cover the road.

⬛

"What's that *suyapo* doing here?" It's the old man's voice. The two Warm Springs men sitting on the bench beside me, a father and his grown son, look at me. "Don't listen to him." It's the father who speaks. His son nods. They are embarrassed. The father holds a single eagle feather; he will be one of the medicine singers tonight.

"It's all right," I tell them. I understand the old man's anger better than their forgiveness. The children have been stolen. And stolen again. How do you get over that? How can you forgive? The river too, of course. The salmon. The trees, the roots. Everything. Even these ceremonies were stolen, taken away by people whose hands couldn't hold them but took them anyway. The old man can remember when they had to hide behind blackout windows. People went to jail for dancing.

But one of my Indian students had waited after class to invite me here. "My mom wants you to come," she said. "It's a winter dance; it's for healing."

How does her mother know, I wonder? Or does everyone need healing? She had told her mother about me, Starla said. How I include Native writers in the class syllabus. I was so grateful that I could hardly listen to the directions, which Starla was drawing in purple ink. "It's right by the river," she said. "You'll find it. Everyone finds this place."

A woman on the bench behind me now touches my shoulder. An elder. "Come sit up here," she says. I squeeze in beside her. She is married to the man who called me *suyapo*, she says. She wants to know why I'm here. Then she tells me about another child, her daughter, who disappeared twenty-three years ago. Drinking, drugs. Twenty-three years. I can't look at her. We watch the young dancers in the tight circle, their dark hair leaping in the dim light as the room fills with sound.

It's like singing underwater, a chorus of light inside the darkness. These prayers, the elder tells me, are for everyone. For these young dancers, who are struggling right now. For her daughter. For my son, too.

Long after I've forgotten about time, the dancing stops. "Thank you," I say to Starla's mother, Lucinda. "Thank you for inviting me." Tomorrow is my son's birthday, I tell her. The second since he's been gone. "These songs—"

"Tell them," she says. She rings a small bell, and the voices stop. "This is Starla's teacher," she says. "She has something to tell you." I hear my voice, words small as pine needles, floating above the silence of the room. "My son…seventeen…gone and…this healing, for him and…for me…thank you."

"You live with it," Lucinda tells me. I don't understand it, but I too just keep breathing. In and out. Like the two little boys she cares for, who watched as their father followed their mother into the bedroom, holding the knife. "I told that social worker," she says. "I'm not real educated, but I don't think they need to be sticking pins into balloons. They know what happened. We talked about it."

By now I know her house by the river. The door is never locked, and if she finds me waiting on the steps, my fingers deep in the neck fur of the old dog, Lucinda wonders why I haven't just gone inside. It's a rough board house like the one I grew up in. But this is the house that Lucinda's father had pulled down from the Japanese internment camp in the hills just above us after The Dalles Dam flooded Celilo Falls and he had to find a place for his family to live. Two barrack sections, joined together.

How does it feel to hear the floodgates close, to watch the water behind the big new wall of concrete smothering Celilo? You have ridden out over white froth in a swinging cable car with the Gorge wind pushing spray into your face, sharing the ride back to the women waiting on the river bank with a salmon almost as big as you are. Your father and his father, and his, have heard the river roaring a circle around their dreams on Big Island for longer than you can imagine. For 14,000 years Celilo has been the center of life, the heart of culture in the Northwest. The point of balance between men's roles and women's, between people and animals, water and fire. I think of London, casually flooded. Or Rome, becoming Atlantis. I try to imagine leaving the river that day. When the swallows flew upriver next spring, who would be there to greet them? Who would know their language? Not even your grandmother will be able to keep you from the Catholic boarding school at Warm Springs, where you will be number twenty-five in the morning line to use the bathroom.

The voices that gather around Lucinda's long table are quiet. Sometimes there is laughter, often silence. Always, outside, I can hear the river. On Sunday morning there is a dish of roots cooked with salmon that I hold inside my mouth, savoring the taste for a long time before I swallow. I remember the Ice Age story of the fight between the wolves and the salmon, eternal ice and the flow of the seasons. The wolves destroy all the salmon, even all of the salmon eggs: all but one, small and shriveled, stuck in a crack of rock too deep for their licking tongues. This one is washed out by the spring rains, slips downriver to the grandmother who waits to nurture him, teach him, send him back....

Little swimmer. I remember my son's small, slick body, his underwater smile. I remember pushing him up for a breath of air.

Fewer and fewer salmon are making it past the dams this year. One man shakes his head. "Yeah, they gotta have their power." It's a bitter joke. Just past the serviceberry bush, at the edge of the still-swift Deschutes, is the sweathouse. Another kind of power.

When the meal is over, it ends as it has begun, with water. "Chuus." Everyone pushes back from the table.

I speak his name aloud, sometimes, as if it will keep him alive. *Josh. Joshua.* People blink, turn away. "It would be easier if you knew he was dead," they say. One woman urges me to have a laying-to-rest ceremony for him.

When the army followed the Navajos into Canyon de Chelly, I remember reading, some escaped capture and the long walk south to the killing place, the concentration camp at Bosque Redondo. Every day these people climbed the hills and spoke the names of the missing ones aloud. Four years later, some of them—the ones left alive—came home.

On PBS, they're talking about the rivers again. Floyd Dominy says he's sorry they didn't dam every river. All that wasted power! David Brower, who stopped the avalanche of dams and even the dam in the center of the Grand Canyon, believes he's a failure because he didn't stop the Glen Canyon dam. A woman begins to cry. She had looked up at the cathedral rock formation, she says, from the bottom of Glen Canyon; in her boat on the dam's reservoir later, she would look down at a faint glint in the water and realize it was the cathedral, buried, still catching the light.

But the Glen Canyon dam, another old river-runner reminds us, will eventually disappear. Like the other sixteen basalt-flow dams that have plugged the Canyon. See? You can read it in the canyon walls. One by one, these stone dams have cracked under the river's need to flow. Vanished.

It just takes time, he says.

How many salmon make it back up the river? I understand the odds. It has been two years now. But he's not dead. I can feel him, under my heart. I will know, I tell myself, if he dies. And he comes to me, now, in dreams. His skin is incredibly warm, his voice softened by love. "I need to stay here a while longer," he tells me.

One morning I wake just at sunrise with the light from my dream spreading into the curtain and the dew-whitened grass of the back yard. I have seen the sacred earth, lit from within, a golden light. The arched bodies of gods, long and narrow like Rainbow God, held up the hills. "All the earth is sacred," said the voice beside me, inside me. "Here, they can see the gods in the earth because they know this. But it's sacred where you stand, too."

The dream stays with me, floating behind my eyes. I'm walking beside the North Fork—just a narrow creek now in the August heat—when I see them. They arch, splashing the shallow water into the sun. Spring Chinook: silver and black, their bodies scarred and torn. Their battered heads turn upstream, into the current. The male chases a trout as it darts from the bank, eager for a taste of her eggs.

There's a lot of talk now about breaching the dams, digging channels to let the river flow around them. Even removing some dams, the ones upstream. We'll have to decide, other people say. The cost, they add, might be too high. After all, it's just a fish.

Meantime, against all odds, a few salmon batter their way through. I watch the water, waiting. You have to be ready to welcome them, I know, or they will quit coming back to us forever.

Bette Lynch Husted's work has appeared in *Fourth Genre, Northern Lights, Northwest Review* and other magazines.

This essay was the third-place winner in the 2001 *Oregon Quarterly* Northwest Perspectives Essay Contest. It is part of a memoir, *Above the Clearwater.*

The Untellable Story

John Daniel

How this view of the truth could lessen anyone's adoring
reverence of the Infinite Source of all this wider force and
profounder power is difficult to understand.
— Thomas Condon 1822–1907, a Christian Darwinist
and a founding faculty member of the University of
Oregon

I don't remember when or how the concept of evolution first entered
my awareness, but it probably came as history rather than biology. My
father, who had been a socialist in the 1930s, still liked to think in terms
of the Marxian dialectic as I was growing up, so it's likely I absorbed at an
early age a sense that historical progress is a function of struggles between
opposite forces. I seem to remember my father telling me about the Scopes
trial—Clarence Darrow was one of his heroes—but the issue as argued at
the trial was pretty crude, and my grasp of it even cruder. It seemed there
were two possibilities. Humans had been created by the God of the Bible,
or humans had descended from apes. (Who had created the apes, or what
they had descended from, I don't recall hearing.) Some of my boyhood
friends belittled the descent-from-apes theory, and I very likely belittled it
too. It wasn't comfortable or even very plausible to young boys with
noticeable hair only on their heads, though I do remember the thought
of it crossing my mind once in the dressing room of the community

swimming pool as I watched a thoroughly hairy man take off his clothes and pull on his trunks.

My friends and I were familiar with the phrase "survival of the fittest," and it was by that phrase that we understood, or misunderstood, evolution. My interest in Jack London's novels must have strengthened the notion that only the strongest survive, and only through bloody struggle. This did not bode well for a quiet kid who liked books and hated to fight, so I didn't think about it much. Just because it might be true for dogs and wolves, I reasoned, and maybe for poor workers and rich bosses, didn't mean it was true for me.

It's hard to believe that the topic of evolution never came up in eighth-grade science or ninth-grade biology, but if it did I don't recall it. Maybe the subject was still too charged for teachers and textbooks in the early 1960s. Though I was aware that people disagreed strongly on the question of human origins, I had no strong feelings of my own. I was raised with some exposure to the theology and imaginal flavor of Christianity, but no practice of it other than a few sessions of Unitarian Sunday school and an occasional midnight service at one church or another on Christmas Eve. The first few lines of Genesis, the Twenty-third Psalm, and portions of the Gospels were the only parts of the Bible I would have recognized. I had a brief love affair with the Christ story when I was fourteen, but my emotional intensity quickly backslid into fishing, baseball and eventually girls. In the absence of a religious faith or a scientific understanding of evolution, I didn't dwell on human origins. When I looked beyond the busy and problematic present, I looked always forward, toward the uncertain but tantalizing future, and toward my personal future, the only one that really counted.

It was Loren Eiseley, in *The Immense Journey,* who first showed me the vastness of time and made me feel part of the evolutionary work of time. His book, which I came to while in high school, moved me not because he explained evolution—he didn't—but because he imagined it. He put the theory into images and the images into a story, an epic narrative in which humankind was only one character. It didn't bother me a bit to learn that we may have descended from a small, rodentlike mammal that burrowed in the ground, a "shabby little Paleocene rat, eternal tramp and world wanderer, father of all mankind." I liked having that guy in my lineage—it was like having an unsavory and quite colorful great-uncle in the family. Because of him I felt a little closer to the woodchucks and squirrels I saw on my Blue Ridge rambles and even learned a little respect for Uncle Tom, the rat who was a permanent tenant and true proprietor of our cabin in those northern Virginia mountains. And I liked it that this great-uncle's own great-uncles had evaded by night the towering reptiles—or evaded them frequently enough, in any case—and that even earlier ancestors had spent fifty million years or so in "the green twilight of the rain forest," acquiring hands that gripped and eyes that focused as one and saw the world in color. The story of evolution shed light on many things, including my childhood love of climbing trees.

That Eiseley was a paleontologist strengthened his authority, but it was the saga, not the science, that excited me. He provided me—and, I'm sure, many others without religious belief—with a creation narrative. Or better, an emergence narrative. Eiseley, like Darwin before him, didn't claim to know or to be able to know the origin of life. In this way their evolution story resembles those Native American tales that presuppose the existence of a raw world and tell how humans emerged out of and into that world—ascending through a series of underground rooms in the Zuni story, issuing from a hollow log in the Kiowa version. Evolution also imagines life emerging from the planet's womb—coalescing somehow as simple forms in the ocean deeps, proliferating throughout the seas, making landfall eventually and colonizing the continents and producing in time as part of its prodigious array at least one species able to look back and wonder at the story and try to piece it together from the incomplete evidence available.

Eiseley led my imagination not just to the evolution of life but to the older and vaster stories of geology and cosmology. The big bang theory was getting a lot of attention as I grew up, suggesting strongly that not only life on Earth but the physical universe itself was an evolutionary

John Daniel

phenomenon, originating from a single source and developing over the course of thousands of millions of years. Somehow, it began to occur to me, every story must live within other stories, from grains of sand on the Carolina coast to the sun and moon to the farthest stars and beyond, and all must be encompassed in one infinite story. Though I couldn't grasp or define that story, or even the smaller ones that composed it, I knew I believed in it, and though I still can't grasp or define it, I believe in it now. Science and religion and poetry show flashes of it. In Nature I sense the story everywhere and beauty is the best name I know for it. I don't mean grace or symmetry or sublimity or any other particular measure of beauty, but all of those and more—the beauty of wholeness, of stars and land and the forms of life precisely as Nature has made them and is making them now, the beauty that Emily Dickinson called "nature's fact." This is the oldest beauty, the beauty essential to the meaning of the Greek term *kosmos*, the beauty whose derivation as a word relates it to "bounty" and ultimately to the Sanskrit *duvas*, meaning "reverence" or "gift." The beauty of the given world. The beauty that is always a becoming, life and death both dancing to it, one long and varied gesture reaching through time.

Evolution has become my faith, and I mean that word in its full religious significance. To have faith is to trust with confidence in the unseen. I trust the unseen movement of being by which the universe gave birth to our sun and planet, by which they gave birth to life, and by which life has elaborated into a diverse wholeness we are only beginning to know. There is strong evidence supporting evolution as scientific theory, but believing in evolution as I imagine it is still a matter of faith. I have never seen one species of life transform into another. I can't prove that the homologous forelimbs of amphibians and birds and bats and whales and humans all derive from a common ancestor, or that the development of the human embryo recapitulates the evolutionary metamorphosis of fish into amphibian into reptile into mammal. I can't prove that I like to climb trees and am physiologically equipped for it because epochs ago my great-great-uncles lived off the ground in African forests.

And, needless to say, neither I nor anyone else has performed the neat trick of turning a beaker of amino acids into a living creature. Charles Darwin acknowledged and evidently was untroubled by his own unscientific faith concerning ultimate origins. "There is grandeur in this view of life," he wrote in *The Origin of Species*, "having been originally breathed by the Creator into a few forms or into one," from which "endless forms most beautiful and most wonderful have been, and are being evolved." Loren Eiseley cited no Creator as author of the evolutionary journey, but confessed his own faith in a "mysterious principle known as 'organization'": "Like some dark and passing shadow within matter, it cups out the eyes' small windows or spaces the notes of a meadowlark's song in the interior of a mottled egg. That principle—I am beginning to suspect— was there before the living in the deeps of water."

Any account of the origin of life or the origin of being, whether religious or scientific or a blend of both, is necessarily an imagining of faith. The biblical story of Genesis is one such imagining, a beautiful one that shapes my life and work, I am sure, in more ways than I know. I admire its orderly progression, the sure and stately way it depicts an evolution of its own. God calls forth light from darkness, heaven and dry land from the formless waters, grasses and herbs and fruit trees from the land, swimming and flying creatures from the oceans and cattle and other terrestrial animals "after their kinds" from the fresh and green-growing earth. All of this is good in the eyes of God, but only humans are specifically said to have been made in God's image. I've always stumbled on that part of the story. In my late twenties, five unexceptional words in the writings of C. G. Jung rang my spirit like a bell: "God wants to become man," he wrote, referring to the Christ story. Not man, I thought, but God wants to *become*. God materializes, incarnates himself in matter, to realize the fullness of his being in the evolving panoply of the cosmos. He did not design the universe but desires it, the way a poet desires the poem he can't yet see and finds its design only in its making. God finds his way only as

John Daniel

we and the rest of creation find ours. And so, being extends itself in ever developing orders of wholeness that form and dissolve in death and then re-form, inhabiting possibility with the amplitude of all that is.

Or so I imagine it, but there are only two things I hold certain. Being is a miracle, and the true nature of the miracle is beyond our knowing. The terms and categories we employ when talking about ultimate things, including "beauty", "wholeness", "God", "evolution", and others I use are crude signifiers, markers made of clay. To speak of mind or matter or design or desire or chance or necessity is to peer through a lens that distorts other regions of the truth as it brings a particular region into focus. In the nineteenth century no one doubted the distinction between matter and energy; now, to physicists at least, that difference has melted. I suspect that other distinctions we habitually assume, including that between the animate and the inanimate, will turn out to tell more about the limits of rational analytic thinking than they tell about the nature of being.

And that's just as well. Like poetry and all art, stories live by suggestion, not explanation, and in that way the greatest story, the story of being, lives in our minds and hearts. To be alive is to hear and tell stories, and the stories are as alive as we are. They change in the hearing and telling. They change as we live on in our lives, as humankind lives farther into time. They will not be restrained in static versions. Maybe the only truly impoverished souls are the rigidly orthodox, whether religious or scientific—those so obsessed with the text of a single story that they deny the validity of others and lose sight of the beauty their own story is meant to suggest, not to contain. The great feast ready before them, they gnaw instead on the meager nourishment of the menu.

"Talk of mysteries!" wrote Thoreau, all stirred up on a Maine mountain. "Think of our life in nature,—daily to be shown matter, to come in contact with it,—rocks, trees, wind on our cheeks! the *solid* earth! the *actual* world!" If you follow the physicists, the actual world is made of willful little particles with names like "quark" and "gluon" that dodge into and out of existence, enlivening a universe born some fifteen billion years ago from a single seed of space and time, an evolving universe that has composed itself into nebulas, stars, planets, and Thoreau with wind on his cheeks. If you follow the Bible or another good book you may imagine the story differently, but whatever the story you see by, the world is here, impossible and undeniable, its own most eloquent explanation. We belong to a mystery that does not belong to us, yet it is freely granted, everywhere and all the time. We distance ourselves, we fail to see, but the mystery does not fail us. It spirals through the molecules of our own DNA, through the shells of snails and the chambered nautilus, through the grain of junipers and the great spinning storms and the spiral arms of the Milky Way, and so joins itself to the infinite from which it arose.

John Daniel, author of six books and two-time winner of the Oregon Book Award for Literary Nonfiction, lives north of Noti, Oregon. He served as judge for the 2002 *Oregon Quarterly* Northwest Perspectives Essay Contest.

This essay appeared in the Summer 2002 issue of *Oregon Quarterly*. It is adapted from his most recent book, *Winter Creek: One Writer's Natural History* (Milkweed Editions, 2002).

The editors wish to thank Tom Hager for the original vision that has guided *Oregon Quarterly*; the University of Oregon for its support of the magazine; Susan Thelen, *Oregon Quarterly*'s advertising director, Chris Michel, designer, and Shelly Cooper, office coordinator, who are intrinsic to all that *Oregon Quarterly* is; Jackie Melvin, our sharp-eyed proofreader; Brett Campbell, assistant editor, who helped in the editing of some of these essays; Jeffrey Flowers, who designed the book, and Jessica MacMurray of the UO Press, who turned the long simmering idea of this book into the reality you hold in your hands.

G.M. & K.H.